SECTION A
Context

Group work is defined, providing the background for all other books in the kit

Other Books in the Group Work Practice Kit

What Is
Group Work?

What Is Group Work?

Robert K. Conyne
*Seattle University and the
University of Cincinnati*

Leann Terry Diederich
*The Pennsylvania
State University*

Los Angeles | London | New Delhi
Singapore | Washington DC

Los Angeles | London | New Delhi
Singapore | Washington DC

FOR INFORMATION:

SAGE Publications, Inc.
2455 Teller Road
Thousand Oaks, California 91320
E-mail: order@sagepub.com

SAGE Publications Ltd.
1 Oliver's Yard
55 City Road
London EC1Y 1SP
United Kingdom

SAGE Publications India Pvt. Ltd.
B 1/I 1 Mohan Cooperative Industrial Area
Mathura Road, New Delhi 110 044
India

SAGE Publications Asia-Pacific Pte. Ltd.
3 Church Street
#10-04 Samsung Hub
Singapore 049483

Copyright © 2014 by SAGE Publications, Inc.

Printed in the United States of America

Library of Congress Cataloging-in-Publication Data

A catalog record of this book is available from the Library of Congress.

9781483332314

This book is printed on acid-free paper.

Acquisitions Editor: Kassie Graves
Editorial Assistant: Elizabeth Luizzi
Production Editor: Brittany Bauhaus
Copy Editor: Megan Granger
Typesetter: C&M Digitals (P) Ltd.
Proofreader: Rae-Ann Goodwin
Indexer: Marilyn Augst
Cover Designer: Anupama Krishnan
Marketing Manager: Shari Countryman

SUSTAINABLE FORESTRY INITIATIVE
Certified Chain of Custody
Promoting Sustainable Forestry
www.sfiprogram.org
SFI-01268
SFI label applies to text stock

13 14 15 16 17 10 9 8 7 6 5 4 3 2 1

Brief Contents _____

_____ Detailed Contents

Acknowledgments_____

Thanks to the SAGE staff for their support, to the book manuscript reviewers for their insight, to all group work practitioners for their dedication and contributions, to my coauthor, Leann, for her great ideas, and to my wife, Lynn, for allowing me the freedom to take up such projects in the first place!

—Robert K. Conyne

Many thanks to all the group work practitioners who have mentored me throughout the past 10 years; you are too numerous to name but have been instrumental in my development. I value Bob, for his patience and support through this first experience in writing a book, and my husband, David, for helping me laugh and play when life gets a bit too serious.

—Leann Terry Diederich

Group Work Practice Kit Acknowledgments

Thanks to Kassie Graves and the wonderful SAGE team, once again, for their support and guidance. Appreciation to the kit's reviewers, who offered valuable insight in its development: Sally H. Barlow, Brigham Young University; John C. Dagley, Auburn University; Arthur M. Horne, The University of Georgia; Marilyn MacGregor, Western New Mexico University; Niloufer M. Merchant, St. Cloud State University; Chuck Reid, The University of Texas -Pan American; and John L. Romano, University of Minnesota. All the authors in this project merit particular thanks, and I especially value the mentorship provided by the senior authors to their younger coauthors. I am honored for the endorsement of the kit by the Association for Specialists in Group Work. A tip of my hat to all group leaders and those learning to assume that vaunted role. And, finally, I bow deeply and thankfully to my family for all their support and love.

Introduction

The *Group Work Practice Kit: How to Improve the Everyday Practice of Group Work* consists of a collection of brief practice books covering the span of group work application, based on research evidence. Its intent is to provide practitioners, instructors, students, and trainees with concrete direction for spreading and improving group work practice by counselors, psychologists, social workers, student personnel, and other human service personnel.

The kit comprises nine independent books that are presented concisely, intended to be easily readable and to provide usable ideas and directions. These books all address critical practical areas within group work. The emphasis throughout is on creating interesting, scholarly, and pragmatic guidance for planning, performing, and processing group work. Each book is infused with appropriate attention to diversity and multicultural issues, with attention to accreditation and/or specialty standards.

This series is a closed-ended series of books, purchasable in its entirety or as individual books. The kit has been developed to attract interest across a number of disciplines and among practitioners.

The kit's span encompasses major aspects of planning, performing, and processing group work—that is, across the span of group work practice, from conceiving an idea for a group (planning) to delivering it (performing) and then evaluating its conduct and effectiveness (processing). Each book within the kit, however, independently represents a single area of substance.

A unique aspect of this kit is that all senior authors, who are established scholars in the group work field, have teamed up with knowledgeable coauthors who are early career professionals in the field. The intent is to produce solid and innovative products while also nurturing and mentoring (and learning from) these early-stage professionals.

Another special aspect of this kit is that it is endorsed by the Association for Specialists in Group Work (ASGW). In fact, ASGW will receive a designated portion of any royalties generated from the sale of books in the kit.

A third feature of this kit is that all books weave evidence-based information with practical application. In the latter instance, all books include a range of learning exercises aimed at helping readers translate concepts into everyday use and enabling instructors to assist the readers in doing so.

Thumbnail Sketch of Book Contents

Section A. Context

Group work is defined, providing the background for all other books in the kit.

Book 1: What Is Group Work?

Robert K. Conyne and Leann Terry Diederich

This introductory book establishes a general context and framework for the kit and its chapters. It presents an inclusive conception of group work, defines types of groups, connects with extant accreditation and/or specialty standards, demonstrates how best practices in group work and attention to diversity and multicultural issues can be used to guide practice, illustrates how key group processes (e.g., group cohesion) can be used to mobilize effort, and sets the stage for the importance of translating available group work evidence into group leader practice.

Section B. Planning

Effective practice depends on many factors, not the least of which is proper planning and preparation.

Book 2: Effective Planning for Groups

Janice L. DeLucia-Waack and Amy Nitza

Any intentional group is based on a coherent group plan. This book identifies the elements that are basic to any plan and applies these elements within an ongoing example. Among these elements are identifying the population, need and environmental assessment, goals, rationale for using group, type of group, conceptual framework used, attention to group developmental stage and group dynamics, group size, group composition, session-by-session plans, and evaluation methodology.

Book 3: How to Form a Group

Lynn S. Rapin and Jeri L. Crowell

One of the larger challenges in using groups stems from the practical challenges involved in their formation. Environmental roadblocks (e.g., agency staff's lack of support for groups) to group formation are identified and countered with strategic antidotes that work. This book outlines clear strategies to consider for organizing groups and how to attract the "right" members to the "right" groups. Organizing, marketing, recruiting, screening, selecting, and composing groups are concretely addressed, with differential attention to groups that are more remedial in purpose and those that are more preventive in scope.

Section C. Performing

Group leaders need to create with members conditions that serve to empower growth, learning, and change, and they need to deploy leader interventions in a genuine and strategic way.

Book 4: Groups: Fostering a Culture of Change

Cheri L. Marmarosh, Emily Carter Dunton,
and Claudia Amendola

Group leaders need to be "culture-of-change builders." This book identifies group conditions that have evidentiary support. The authors point out how these conditions combine to yield a positive group culture, and they indicate how leaders can nurture and support these conditions.

Book 5: How to Select and Apply Change Strategies in Groups

Ed Jacobs and Christine Schimmel

Group leaders need to develop competencies, functions, and strategies aimed at helping members benefit from a positive group culture as they pursue their own learning. These competencies, functions, and related intervention strategies are detailed in this book.

Section D. Processing

Both group members and leaders learn from experience, but they learn more powerfully from the meaning they derive from their group experience.

Book 6: How to Help Leaders and Members Learn From Their Group Experience

Donald E. Ward and Christopher A. Ward

This book highlights practical ways that leaders can help members learn from their ongoing group experience through guided illumination of selected group events that have recently occurred. It also shows the necessity of group leaders' reflecting on their practice between group sessions (e.g., through supervision) by providing examples and practice exercises.

Book 7: How Leaders Can Assess Group Counseling

Maria T. Riva and Robin E. Lange

Researchers have produced ample evidence that well-planned and well-delivered group work can benefit members. To add to the general storehouse of knowledge and, more important, to continually improve local group work practice, it is desirable that each individual group experience be evaluated for effectiveness as well as for its capacity to meet other criteria (e.g., appropriateness). Practitioners frequently find the evaluation requirement difficult to accomplish due to its assumed complexity. This book provides practical guidance about how to establish—or collaborate with researchers to accomplish—research designs aimed at evaluating group process and outcomes. Group work measures and both quantitative and qualitative approaches are described, with suggestions for group leader use.

Section E. Applying Group Work in the Community and in Schools

Book 8: Groups in Community and Agency Settings

Niloufer M. Merchant and Carole J. Yozamp

Group work is becoming commonplace in community settings, such as in sexual assault centers, mental health centers, battered women's shelters, chemical dependency units, community planning, employee training and development, employee assistance centers, and in other outpatient, inpatient, and residential settings. It even is beginning to occur somewhat more frequently in private practice. This book demonstrates how group work, ranging from remedial through preventive forms, is manifested in an array of community settings, thus providing readers with practical, concrete information about how group work is being used—and can be used even more effectively.

Book 9: Group Work in Schools

John Dagley and Erin English

Schools receive too little attention in the group work literature, but they are settings in which groups play a critically important role—one that can be expanded in the future. This book demonstrates how group work is being used within schools, ranging from elementary through college and university levels. It emphasizes remedial as well as developmental and preventive applications of groups—including psychoeducation group formats—and gives attention to groups having an educational and career focus.

Intended Audiences

The *Group Work Practice Kit: Improving the Everyday Practice of Group Work* is intended for undergraduate courses in the human services and for graduate courses in psychology (counseling, clinical, school, consulting, and community), counselor education (mental health, community, college, and school counseling), education, social work, and student affairs, as well as for the legion of practitioners in the group work field. The intent is to provide pragmatic approaches based on research evidence better to support the effective use of group work. Therefore, both current practitioners and faculty/ students/trainees are prime targets, each category being in strong need of a resource such as that being provided here.

Current practitioners often are asked to deliver groups without having been taught research-based practice methods for forming, leading, and processing them. The limited availability of group work courses in higher education tends to include texts that are conceptual and theoretical in emphasis, without giving sufficient attention to concrete application issues and approaches. This kit provides accessible resources focused on practical application issues and approaches based on research, presented in a highly readable and usable manner, and structured to enhance teaching and learning processes.

This resource is intended to be practical and to provide readers with pragmatic practice directions across the key cycle of group work, from conception to delivery to determining effectiveness. *The goal for the kit and each of its books is to contribute to the improvement of everyday group practice.* The kit, I should think, will be fully useful in its entirety to practitioners, and the design of the selected books within it will cogently supplement required texts assigned in any group-oriented course.

Targeted Professional Associations

Members of a range of associations involved with the helping professions should find the contents of this kit of interest. These associations include American Counseling Association, American Group Psychotherapy Association, American Psychological Association, Association for the Advancement of Group Work, Association of Counselor Education and Supervision, Association for Specialists in Group Work, National Association for Social Workers, National Organization for Human Services, Society of Counseling Psychology, Society of Group Psychology and Group Psychotherapy, and others.

Academic Disciplines

Group work is a multidisciplinary, multiprofession method. In addition to psychology, social work, and counselor education, the kit could serve courses and practitioners in a variety of other disciplines and professions: human services, social work, public health, and health promotion, among others.

Practitioners

A key target audience for this book is practitioners in the field—those who are asked to undertake group work, too often with inadequate training and practical skills. They need focused resources, such as the books in this kit, to guide their thinking and efforts.

1

Ingredients of Group Work

What Practitioners Need to Know and Do

In this first chapter, we will examine the major ingredients of group work, with an eye toward what it is that group practitioners really need to know and be able to do. But first, let's begin by presenting a brief scenario that will guide our discussion and your application.

Guiding Scenario

Imagine that you are a counselor in the university counseling center. This well-respected center is known for excellence in providing individual, direct counseling services to students. A new director is bringing to the center a number of new perspectives and initiatives, with a theme meant to help the center increase its visibility and develop a broader array of services for all members of the university population.

As part of this new approach, group work services are envisioned, and guess what? *You have been named the group work coordinator.* Your assigned task is to develop a plan for instituting a comprehensive group work program for the center that will target the wide range of needs presented by the university population. Keep the above scenario in mind as you read about the ingredients of group work, to follow.

Definition of Group Work

When one is asked to create a plan for a comprehensive group work program, many questions arise. Some of them revolve around program development processes that are necessary to guide program creation (Conyne, 2010), while others relate to understanding the parameters that will be used to define the group work services themselves. These latter matters are what we will focus on in this introductory book.

Our attention will be focused most closely, but not only, on what we term *person-change groups* within group work—counseling, therapy, and psychoeducation. We do this for two reasons: (a) Person-change groups most often are what counselors and other professional helpers are called on to deliver, and (b) most of the knowledge about group work comes from studies of those kinds of groups. Yet, consistent with a comprehensive view of group work, we will encourage you also to consider how the information provided connects with task groups.

As the newly appointed group work coordinator, one of your first tasks is to accumulate the best information about group work services you can, prior to moving ahead with action planning steps. An important first step is to answer this question: "What is comprehensive group work?" Doing so will allow you to project an initial operating framework to suggest to others when moving forward together in designing the overall group work services program.

You begin by posing to yourself a teasing question: "What is it about being in a group that is beneficial?" From personal experience, you know that generally you enjoy being with others because often these experiences can be fun and satisfying. When you've been confronted by a life challenge, such as coping with the recent death of your father, you've frequently found it helpful and supportive to talk with friends and sometimes family members about it; in the case of losing your father, you found becoming involved with group counseling to be additionally helpful. You typically have noticed that working on projects in a group or team, while sometimes frustrating, can yield ideas and solutions you could not have reached alone. You also cannot forget what an older neighborhood couple, Ruby and Oren, said about why they persisted over 35 years, sunny or snowy, to participate in a weekly Saturday afternoon card game: "It's not the card playing we like; it's our friends!" (Conyne, 2004). Further, it turns out from your reading that many of your personal experiences with groups are supported by general research in the scholarly literature (e.g., Forsyth, 2011; Hogg, Hohman, & Rivera, 2008; Kivlighan, Miles, & Paquin, 2011).

Your knowledge of the scholarly literature also supports the use of group approaches. It is important to realize this fact, because the counseling center you represent needs to successfully provide services that both address important local needs and are supported by evidence. It is obvious to most practitioners and policymakers that group methods are efficient because a number of people can be reached and helped simultaneously by just one or two group leaders. Moreover, the research coalesces to indicate that well-designed and well-delivered group work services often are as effective as individually delivered ones, sometimes more so (for summaries, see, for example, Conyne, 2011a, 2011b; DeLucia-Waack, Gerrity, Kalodner, & Riva, 2004).

As you continue conducting background research into the field of group services, you come to an understanding that theorists and practitioners alike have adopted different conceptions of these group services. As in the broader counseling field itself, a commonly accepted definition of the process of counseling has remained elusive over the decades. Yet, on October 28, 2010, the following definition was adopted by the American Counseling Association Governing Council: "Counseling is a professional relationship that empowers diverse individuals, families, and groups to accomplish mental health, wellness, education, and career goals" (American Counseling Association, 2013).

By contrast, it seems to you that any common definition of group services still awaits general agreement. What is meant by the term *group services*? As with counseling itself, are group services intended to accomplish mental health, wellness, education, and career goals? Or are those goals attached solely to group counseling? Should group services be focused on one or several methods? On group counseling? Group psychotherapy? What about other forms of group delivery, such as psychoeducation, support, prevention, or task facilitation? Are they intended to empower, to treat, to prevent? Do they address people who are functioning well or those who are in distress? Or all? Are all these dimensions listed (and perhaps others that are not) to be included? Is it possible that one of the group methods, such as group counseling, might include all the other ones (i.e., group therapy, psychoeducation, etc.)? And, finally, what is meant by "comprehensive group work"?

Considering these issues, you find yourself literally scratching your head in confusion. Yet, the existing professional literature on this topic is fairly robust (for summaries, see Barlow, Burlingame, & Fuhriman, 2000; Barlow, Fuhriman, & Burlingame, 2005; Conyne, 2011a; Ward, 2011) and informative, laying out the various perspectives. However, you find it falls short of the directional clarity you seek. You realize that coming to a position on defining group services through a comprehensive group work approach is necessary for guiding how the counseling center will proceed in that area.

In your research, you come across a number of valuable resources for conceptualizing group approaches and guiding their implementation and evaluation. You note that the American Group Psychotherapy Association's (2007) *Practice Guidelines for Group Psychotherapy: A Cross-Theoretical Guide to Developing and Leading Psychotherapy Groups* is full of excellent, research-based recommendations for creating, conducting, and evaluating psychotherapy groups. Yet you wonder if the focus on psychotherapy groups (depending on how narrowly they are defined) meets the criterion given to you to develop a plan for comprehensive group work. You branch out of the psychology and counseling fields to discover the *Standards for Social Work Practice With Groups,* created by the Association for the Advancement of Social Work with Groups (2005). Aimed at social workers, you find these suggestions to be valuable because they address a wide range of groups (e.g., treatment, psychoeducational, support, community action, and task) in a variety of settings. You immediately see the potential for adapting some of these recommendations to fit a counseling center setting. As a member of the Society for Group Psychology and Group Psychotherapy (of the American Psychological Association), you are aware of the extensive publications and presentations of many of its members and fellows—many of them influential in the broad field of "groups," particularly for attention given to group practice informed by group research (Society of Group Psychology and Group Psychotherapy, 2013).

You then conduct an Internet search to locate resources developed by the Association for Specialists in Group Work (ASGW; see www.asgw.org), a division of the American Counseling Association. As a longtime member of the association, you've been attracted over the years to what seems to you to be its comprehensive perspective on conceptualizing, organizing, and delivering group services, within the lens of the counseling profession. But it's been a while since you've worked with those materials, and you need a refresher.

Perspective of the Association for Specialists in Group Work

You download from the ASGW website three resources that you think might be helpful for clarifying group work and providing some direction for responding to your assignment as the counseling center group work coordinator: (a) *Professional Standards for the Training of Group Workers* (Wilson, Rapin, & Haley-Banez, 2000), (b) *Best Practice Guidelines* (Thomas & Pender, 2008), and (c) *Multicultural and Social Justice Competence Principles for Group Workers* (Singh, Merchant, Skudrzyk, & Ingene, 2012). Of the three documents, the first one, related to professional training standards, seems to hold the most pertinent information for your initial need to better understand a basic definition of group work.

After reading some of the history leading up to the present document (e.g., that it was preceded by documents published in 1983 and 1990), you are reminded that the primary purpose of the current version is to assist in training future group workers, consisting mainly of students in counselor training programs. But you find some of what you are looking for early in this document, where the term *group work* is defined (Wilson et al., 2000, p. 3):

- Group work is a broad professional practice
- involving the application of knowledge and skill in group facilitation
- to assist an interdependent collection of people
- to reach their mutual goals
- which may be intrapersonal, interpersonal, or work-related and may include

- the accomplishment of tasks related to work, education, personal development, personal and interpersonal problem solving,
- or remediation of mental and emotional disorders.

You remember, and go back to find, a quote by George Gazda (1978) written more than three decades ago, which seems prescient in light of the ASGW training standards:

Group work refers to the dynamic interaction between collections of individuals for prevention or remediation of difficulties or for the enhancement of personal growth/enrichment through the interaction of those who meet together for a commonly agreed-on purpose and at prearranged times. (p. 260)

The elements of the ASGW definition are attractive to you because of their breadth and how that condition fits with the assignment you've been given: "to develop a plan for instituting a comprehensive group work program for the center that will target the wide range of needs presented by the university population." You recall that the new director emphasized that *comprehensiveness* is very important. You decide to take each of the definition's elements and draft your understanding of what each might entail as a step toward creating a proposal for consideration by counseling center staff.

What Each Element of the Group Work Definition Means

- *Broad professional practice.* To you, this element means that group work is somehow inclusive; it is wider than it is narrow. And it's a practice conducted by professionals, which suggests that there is a body of knowledge and skills and some sort of regulation attached.
- *Application of knowledge and skill in group facilitation.* The function, "group facilitation," strikes you as interesting. Again, it seems broad, unrestricted to more specialized functions such as group counseling or group psychotherapy, or even group leadership or group training. Rather, group facilitation is a responsive and adaptive function, one that suggests guiding and supporting as opposed to directing and pre-scribing actions. The knowledge and skills making up group facilita-tion are of value and can most likely be taught and learned (Conyne, Wilson, & Ward, 1997).
- *To assist an interdependent collection of people.* Here you notice the concept of interdependence. Group work, then, promotes the connec-tions among group members. This reminds you of a network or web. The group leader assists members through the interconnections among them that are created and maintained, rather than seeking to direct and control what occurs from the top down (Clanton Harpine, 2013).

- *To reach their mutual goals.* Group work is intentional and goal driven (Conyne, Newmeyer, & Crowell, 2008), where goal accomplishment matters. Moreover, these goals are arrived at through some sort of mutual process. This notion of mutuality, you imagine, is associated with the previous emphasis on interdependence. You like the feel of these concepts—they suggest a kind of "psychological connective tissue" developing through group work that serves to facilitate member interactions and contributes to positive outcomes.
- *(Mutual goals) may be intrapersonal, interpersonal, or work-related.* So, you realize, goals can vary. They can be centered within members, between and among members, or related to how members interact with others outside the group itself, or goals can be geared toward work issues. You are excited about this, thinking of the counseling center and the range of opportunities that might become possible for group work.
- *Goals may include accomplishment of work tasks, education, personal development, personal and interpersonal problem solving, or remediation of mental and emotional disorders.* This aspect of the group work definition further specifies the range of goals that are suitable for group work. The excitement builds for you! Group work, it appears, can be used to improve work settings, to help individuals develop and grow, to solve interpersonal issues, to improve interpersonal skills, and to correct psychological and emotional disorders.

As you ponder your understanding of this definition of group work, it seems entirely possible that a group work program could be developed that would reach out to a broad campus audience. Groups could be provided that might help organizations function better (e.g., student organizations), help students gain personal and interpersonal skills that might serve to prevent future problems, and help presently troubled students reduce and correct dysfunctions. In fact, this kind of approach would seem to satisfy the need for comprehensiveness.

Learning Exercise _____

Begin a proposal about a comprehensive group work program.

The goal of this learning exercise is to further your understanding of what may be contained in a comprehensive group work program.

Respond to the three items below to help define a comprehensive group work program.

Now that you are developing an idea of what a comprehensive group work program might consist of, let's take it a step further and put this idea in writing. Doing so, you know, will help further clarify your own thinking and could form the beginnings of a proposal you can present to the director and then to other staff. Follow the structure below to help you get started with a proposal you might be able to share later.

a. *Define the needs you are trying to address in the program:*

_____

_____

_____

b. *Identify three desired outcomes of the program:*

1. _____

2. _____

3. _____

c. *Describe the program's essential components and how they can be expected to be comprehensive.*

_____

_____

_____

Group Work Types

You now have a start on conceiving a comprehensive group work program. But you know you need to get more specific. How are these comprehensive goals to be reached? What sorts of modalities might be included within the umbrella term of *group work*?

As you read further in the training standards document (and other sources, such as Barlow, 2012; Falls, 2009; and Newmeyer, 2009), you find that different types of group work are described. Each type expands on core, or foundation, competencies that are assumed to be minimally necessary for any form of group work to be conducted adequately. Core competencies include those in group process, group dynamics, group leadership, observation and interpersonal skills, and other areas. You make a note to be sure to develop a procedure that could be used by counseling center staff to assess their level of group work competency, including in the core foundation and in the advanced types of group work application.

According to the ASGW training standards, the distinct types of group work, each demanding advanced specialty training, are

a. task and work group facilitation,

b. psychoeducation group leadership,

c. group counseling, and

d. group psychotherapy.

Task and Work Group Facilitation

This group work type addresses work settings and/or the accomplishment of work tasks within other types of groups (Hulse-Killacky, Killacky, & Donigian, 2001). Group-based educational, developmental, and systemic strategies are applied in the group to promote the efficient and effective accomplishment of task goals. These kinds of goals generally relate to practices, performance, procedures, products, and people (Conyne, Rapin, & Rand, 1997). In addition to core competencies, task group facilitators need specialized knowledge and skills in program development and evaluation, consultation, and organization development. You can see that task and work groups would fit well with counseling center staff who may consult with or train personnel in university departments and agencies and in student organizations. Task group facilitation can be important, too, when they are asked to consult on or lead task forces, planning committees, discussion groups, learning groups, and other related task-oriented groups (Wheelan, 2004).

Brief Task Group Illustration

Context: First meeting of high school task force on reducing obesity

Leader (Sally):   "It's really good to see all of you here tonight. As you know, we've been called together by Principal Schumm to develop a plan to be considered for reducing obesity among all members of our school community, not just our students. We have about 3 months to accomplish this goal. It's a big task, don't you think? But it's really an important one. Before we start to tackle this, though, let's begin by going around the table and introducing ourselves by name, and then saying what constituencies we are representing. We will, of course, need to work together, using all our resources, to get the job done well. Then we'll move toward trying to clarify our charge and see what we need to do to begin meeting it. Okay, let's just go clockwise, starting with . . ."

Commentary: The nuggets of a task group are contained in this brief introduction by the task group leader. Sally makes it clear that this is a working group, lays out the general task at hand and general end point, and then begins to draw members in by asking them to introduce themselves. Although the latter step may seem patently obvious to most readers, it is surprising how many groups like this one are formed with no attempt to help members become acquainted or get generally oriented. Rather, it's often "Okay, let's get to work!" As with all groups, task groups must appropriately integrate the task or content with personal relations to be successful, a point that Sally also makes.

Psychoeducation Group Leadership

This type of group draws from principles of normal human development and functioning, using group-based educational and developmental strategies, to promote personal and interpersonal growth, aid in development, and prevent future difficulties. These groups typically involve some modicum of structure housing an appropriate blend of information dissemination while harnessing group processes. Qualifying members for psychoeducation groups may be at risk for future development of personal or interpersonal problems or may be those who seek enhancement of personal qualities and abilities. You can immediately envision the significant use of psychoeducation groups on campus, both to teach coping skills and to help prevent the occurrence of psychological problems. Groups for stress management, study skills, interpersonal skills, conflict resolution, and many other topics quickly come to mind as possibilities.

Brief Psychoeducation Group Illustration

Context: The fourth of eight sessions in a stress management group

Leader: "Breathing is so obvious, but many of us ignore how we are doing it—or even if we are breathing properly. Especially when under high stress, many people forget to breathe or do so shallowly and swiftly. Much better is to remember to breathe and to do this through the diaphragm and nose, slowly and intentionally—taking in air for four counts and letting it out for four counts. This has the effect of calming the nervous system and the mind, permitting greater access to critical thinking and decision-making processes. So let's give this a try, shall we?"

(The leader then provides specific practice instruction for this form of centered, calming breathing.)

Commentary: A psychoeducation group leader frequently delivers brief "lecturettes" about a pertinent psychoeducational topic or skill and then may ask the members to apply it, usually after a demonstration of how it is done correctly. In this case, the topic and skill is relaxation through breathing. Once members try a skill, a period of feedback may follow, including support geared toward continuing what is working and suggestions for making improvements.

These groups are not all about learning and practicing skills, though. It is also important for open-ended dialogue to occur, with attention to group process, just as in any other group.

Group Counseling

You notice that group counseling and group psychotherapy are separated in these standards. Maybe that makes sense, but you decide you need to think about that one more. At any rate, the ASGW standards position group counseling as addressing everyday personal and interpersonal problems of living, drawing from principles of normal human development and group-based strategies that could be based on cognitive, affective, behavioral, or systemic theories. Group counseling clientele are thought to be experiencing transitory maladjustment or expected life challenges for which personal and interpersonal growth and interpersonal problem solving could be helpful. You can see where group counseling could be a mainstay of any group work program, because it seems to occupy a centrist position, being both problem and growth oriented.

Brief Group Counseling Illustration

Context:	Toward the end of a 20-session counseling group
Group member (Andrea):	"I've been working all these weeks, I guess, on becoming more present, more real, with all of you. It's been a problem my whole life, ya know. I'm a planner, a schemer, and I'm always thinking ahead and behind and around everything, livin' in my head and almost never, as I've learned, connecting with what's right in front of me. Like here in this group, bein' with all of you and not livin' totally in my noggin. Damn, it's hard for me, but I've been tryin' extra hard, and I'm wondering now, before we get out of here in a couple of weeks, about how you all think I'm doin' and about what I could do better even? Whew, *that* took some doin', boy, gettin' *that* out, right here and right now!"
Leader:	"So, Andrea, you're asking us all for feedback about how we see what you've been doing. That's great! Good for you! And, maybe, what you might do even better, you said. I wonder if you might also want to look at what you might be able to take out of here to your world once the group is over?"

Commentary: Here you see the essence of group counseling. Learning from group interaction vital aspects of one's interpersonal functioning, giving and getting feedback, and looking at how learning might be applied.

Group Psychotherapy

With this group type, you note for the only time that both principles of normal and abnormal human development are needed. This is so
because, according to these standards, psychotherapy groups are intended
for those who presently are experiencing significant impairment in their
daily functioning—manifested independently, with other people, and with
tasks. This dysfunctional behavior may be chronic or severe and is disruptive
and negative. You realize that many college students today experience serious and persistent life challenges, beyond a need for personal growth or
interpersonal problem solving surrounding typical life issues; they need
deeper help. This is where psychotherapy groups would be pertinent. You
decide that whether you choose to separate counseling and psychotherapy
groups or combine them, groups need to be made available to help students
and others deal more effectively with typical life challenges and more significant sources of dysfunction.

Brief Group Psychotherapy Sample

Context: Middle point of a 25-session psychotherapy group conducted in the community health clinic

*Group
member
(Austin):* "I gotta say it, I just can't STAND myself." (His voice rises
to a crescendo.) "I look into the mirror and want to break
it in little pieces. One time I actually did that, it's a wonder
I didn't cut my arteries! I don't know where to turn sometimes. Not my family, that's for damn sure, not with them
knowing now that I'm gay. I just feel like an absolute out-
cast. I'm trying to come to terms with all this, but . . ."

Leader: "Austin, thank you for saying this so clearly. Really, that's a
wonderful beginning for you now in the group, letting us in
on some of your thinking, your anger, your fears. That's
exactly why we all are here—to be there for one another. To
listen, to help however we can do that. But first we have to
be honest enough with one another to let us know what's
really going on in our lives. And Austin, I know it hurts, but
this is a big step for you in here."

Commentary: In group psychotherapy, members are hurting, often deeply.
The group exists to provide a supportive and healing forum, a safe place
where people can repair. In this example, the group must be progressing
positively, as Austin now is able to let some of his inner insecurities out, taking a concrete step toward the hope of getting better.

Learning Exercises _____

1. Refer to the group psychotherapy illustration, just above, involving Austin. Try to place yourself as a member who, indeed, has your own problems. But let's assume you are moved, or asked by the group leader, to respond to Austin and what he has just shared. What might you say to him that you think would be helpful?

    a. Write that statement: _____

    _____

    _____ .

    b. Share your statement with a partner. Discuss what you both came up with and what you think might be the effect of each (10 minutes).

2. Start work on creating fliers for each group work type.

The goal of this learning exercise is to advance your understanding of the four group work types described in the ASGW training standards.

Imagine you are just getting started creating fliers that will be sent to academic departments and other campus agencies to describe the types of group work the center will provide.

Translate what you've read about each of these group work types into language that might be acceptable to your audiences. Provide the following information:

  a. *Needs addressed by the group work type*

  b. *Definition of each type*

  c. *How group members might be expected to benefit from each type*

Task groups:

  a. _____

    _____ .

  b. _____

    _____ .

  c. _____

    _____ .

Psychoeducation groups:

  a. _____

    _____ .

b. _____

_____ .

c. _____

_____ .

Counseling groups:

a. _____

_____ .

b. _____

_____ .

c. _____

_____ .

Psychotherapy groups:

a. _____

_____ .

b. _____

_____ .

c. _____

_____ .

3. Give a brief presentation.

Pick *one* of the four group work types, and develop a 3-minute oral presentation you might give to members of a campus student organization as a way to make the offering known for their potential use.

Pick a partner. Take turns giving and critiquing the presentations. In your critique, provide constructive comments that are intended to sharpen the presentations and make them maximally acceptable to the student audience (5 minutes for each round of critiques).

_____ **Summary**

You feel as though you're getting a better handle on what group work is like, in general, and especially on what a broad application of it might be. Now you are becoming more aware of a nagging question, one that other staff no doubt will ask: "Does it work?"

2

Evidence of Group Work Effectiveness

Meaning for Practitioners

As the group work coordinator, you know that a key component to creating a strong group program is to be able to highlight the effectiveness of groups. You've talked to some staff members and learned they believe in the power of groups to create positive changes for clients, but you have also heard some doubts as to the effectiveness of groups. Some concerns you have heard from staff members include the following: "Won't just putting eight people in the room with the same problem make them all worse?" "Isn't group just a way to do individual therapy with more people at the same time?" "Unless group is really intensive, like on an inpatient unit, it won't create any changes." "I wouldn't feel comfortable running a group with both men and women in it. I'd only want to run single-gender groups, because it's the only way people are going to feel safe enough to talk."

You're glad the staff at the counseling center are openly discussing their fears and concerns about group. These may be similar to concerns students might have, so the staff need to be able to have solid answers to them if they are going to make appropriate referrals and lead effective groups. You decide to go to the research literature to see if you can answer some of these questions.

Quantitative Studies

Rather than looking at individual studies, you start by going to a meta-analysis on group work. A *meta-analysis* is a method of aggregating research studies from a wide range of sources (e.g., journals and dissertations) through statistical analysis (Whiston & Li, 2011). In a meta-analysis, the statistical analysis is based on data from each individual study and often results in an effect size. The effect size "serves as a standardized quantitative metric" (p. 274) in meta-analyses and provides an index of the strength of the association between two or more variables. Whiston and Li provided guidelines for using effect sizes in meta-analytic research in counseling, and you file their article away in case your colleagues have some questions on the procedures used in meta-analytic studies.

Person-Change Groups

You decide to focus your attention mostly on person-change groups (i.e., counseling, psychotherapy, and psychoeducation), because that is where you envision getting started with the staff and also because most initial demand will be for those groups. As you read the first meta-analysis in your stack, you start with the article by Burlingame, Fuhriman, and Mosier (2003), which traces the history of group effectiveness research. It provides an interesting backdrop to the more recent studies. In the 1960s, the research allowed for a conclusion that group was a "helpful adjunctive treatment" (p. 3). You chuckle as you realize that group was not even considered a standalone treatment then. The research continued in the 1970s, showing that group outcomes were better than those obtained from controls. The lack of specificity in group research in the 1980s led to calls for a conceptual framework for what are often referred to as *change mechanisms* in groups (Burlingame et al., 2003)—those processes that account for change and growth in members, or in task groups, for creating useful products. In terms of person-change groups, group protocols were developed in the 1990s that focused on specific sets of clients, settings, and analysis of differing orientations of group work practice. Burlingame et al. described the trend for research on specific disorders continuing into the 2000s (for examples, see Choate & Henson, 2003; Oei & Browne, 2006; Sapia, 2001), as well as a focus on cost and efficacy concerns raised by health maintenance organizations (HMOs).

From their meta-analysis of 111 studies from the previous 20 years, Burlingame et al. (2003) concluded that the average group client is better off than 72% of the controls who were untreated. You file this number away to pass on to your staff. You find it encouraging that of their studies, 52% were in a university or college counseling center. This supports the generalizability of their findings to your population. You continue analyzing their study and learn that the effect size for "active treatment," or the comparison from pregroup to postgroup, was statistically significant, with an effect size of 0.71 (Burlingame et al., 2003). This is above the cutoff for the recommended minimum effect size for a "practically significant effect for social science data" (Ferguson, 2009, p. 533). You find it particularly encouraging that the pre- to posttreatment effect sizes for varying diagnoses, including three that are seen quite commonly at your center, were all significant: depression (ES = 1.10), anxiety disorders (ES = 0.84), and eating disorders (ES = 1.38, representing a moderate effect; Ferguson, 2009). You want to offer groups to address all these disorders, and the evidence supports the use of group for these populations. You note that there were no differences found in pre- to posttreatment measurements based on client gender or age.

You do not restrict your literature review to just meta-analyses and come across several other interesting studies. You learn about several psychoeducational group programs; one is for mothers who are survivors of domestic violence and their children (McWhirter & McWhirter, 2010). They compared several methods of providing psychoeducational groups to the women and children. One of them was a goals-focused group (as compared with an emotions-focused group). In the goals-focused group, they helped the women decrease nonadaptive or increase adaptive coping. The three categories of goals were personal (e.g., increasing awareness of feelings), relational (e.g., building healthier bonds with family members), and functional (e.g., drinking less). This seems like a useful set of categories for quick classification of goals, so you take note of it to include in your presentation for staff on what the group program could accomplish. The second set of psychoeducational programs they described is school-based prevention groups, such as SCARE (Student Created Aggression Replacement Education; Herrmann & McWhirter, 2001), SOAR (Students Optimistic Attitudes and Resiliency Program; Gilboy, McWhirter, & Wallace, 2002), ART (Anxiety Reduction Training; Boewe & McWhirter, 2002), and BLOCKS (Building Lives on Companion Knowledge Skills; Fair & McWhirter, 2002). These groups range from primary (methods of prevention undertaken before any problems or dysfunction starts) to tertiary (methods used to mitigate and reduce the impact of problems) prevention programs (McWhirter & McWhirter, 2010). You continue reading about other group approaches that are commonly used in schools, such as the Olweus Bully Prevention Program (Olweus & Limber, 2002) and Bully Busters (Newman-Carlson & Horne, 2004). With the increase in group prevention programs at elementary, middle, and high schools, you wonder if you'll start seeing more students who have experienced group work in the past.

To get an idea of the variety of research findings, you return to the meta-analyses of group work that have been conducted in the past decade. Payne and Marcus (2008) found that group interventions, particularly those that were cognitive-behaviorally based (rather than using reminiscence therapy) were effective for reducing symptoms in older adults (55 years or older). You learn that group treatments are effective for incarcerated offenders across all outcomes analyzed (i.e., anger, depression, institutional adjustment, etc.), even with half the group members mandated to be in group therapy (Morgan & Flora, 2002). Morgan and Flora found that groups that included homework assignments had more positive outcomes, and they concluded that an integrative approach that uses cognitive-behavioral techniques and homework assignments is appropriate for this population. You decide to investigate what might be appropriate homework assignments for some of the psychoeducational groups typically run in college counseling centers and make a note to pose this to the Groupsinscc (groups in college counseling centers) listserv (subscriptions are available at https://lists.fsu.edu/mailman/listinfo/groupsinscc).

You return to the earlier study you were reading that investigated client improvement in group with regard to differences in treatment (e.g., orientation, size, group composition), therapist, client, and methodological variables (Burlingame et al., 2003). They found that members in mixed-gender groups did better than those in single-gender groups. This was supported by a meta-analysis analyzing the effects of psychodrama techniques in groups, which found that mixed-gender groups had higher effect sizes as well (Kipper & Ritchie, 2003). Burlingame et al. (2003) found that clients in homogeneous groups (i.e., homogeneity of client problems) improved more than clients in heterogenous groups. You make note to pass this along to your colleagues as support for using topic-specific groups, such as groups for depression, anxiety, and grief/loss. This seems to be a common trend in college counseling centers, with a number of topic-specific groups often being offered, along with population-specific (e.g., students on the autism spectrum, veterans, international students, and women/men of color) and general interpersonal process groups.

Most of the studies you have been reading are from outpatient settings. Burlingame et al. (2003) found that members in outpatient groups improved more than those in inpatient groups. A different meta-analysis of just inpatient group therapy reported a mean effect size from pre- to posttreatment of 0.59 (Kösters, Burlingame, Nachtigall, & Strauss, 2006). Interestingly, 60% of the studies in the inpatient analysis were done in Germany. One final conclusion from Burlingame et al. that you find interesting is their hypothesis about the combination of findings; that is, *outpatient, homogeneous, and groups with a behavioral orientation are associated with greater client improvement.* This fits a large number of the types of groups your staff will be running and leaves you feeling hopeful about being able to relate the evidence supporting the utilization of groups for your counseling center.

As you conclude with the most recent review, you are pleased to see that the research supporting group treatment has only gotten stronger. Burlingame, Strauss, and Joyce (2013) concluded that the research in the past decade has

> continued to provide clear support from group treatment with good or excellent evidence for most mood disorders reviewed (panic, social phobia, OCD, eating disorders, substance abuse, trauma-related disorders, breast cancer, schizophrenia and personality disorders) and promising for others (mood, pain/somatoform, inpatient). (p. 664)

They also examined the comparative effectiveness of group versus individual treatment format. They concluded that there is no difference between individual and group treatments for mood disorders, panic disorders, personality disorders, schizophrenia, OCD (obsessive-compulsive disorder), eating disorders, and substance-related disorders. However, there are contradictory findings regarding the most effective format for some trauma-related disorders and social phobia (Burlingame et al., 2013). While less relevant to your setting in a college counseling center, you appreciate their citations that examine the cost-effectiveness of group, compared with medication management and individual therapy (see Otto, Pollack, & Maki, 2000; Roberge, Marchand, Reinharz, & Savard, 2008).

You also want to incorporate evidence that focuses on specific techniques, and you return to the meta-analysis that analyzed psychodrama techniques (Kipper & Ritchie, 2003). They found a moderate effect size for the studies included in their analysis, with a Cohen's adjusted *d* coefficient of .95. Of the techniques analyzed, they found that role reversal and doubling showed large effect sizes. They concluded that separate psychodrama techniques such as these could be integrated into other forms of group work (Kipper & Ritchie, 2003). You want to make sure these techniques are incorporated only into groups where the leaders have appropriate competence, and you decide to ask your colleagues if any of them have training in psychodrama.

A Qualitative Approach

Knowing you have focused most of your research review on quantitative outcome studies, you shift your focus to examine a *qualitative* review that examined the process of interactions between group members. Compared with the earlier studies you read that used objective measures, such as surveys and questionnaires, qualitative research uses the researcher as the data-gathering instrument. In this way, the researcher (often with other researchers who act as "auditors" for the analysis) has an ongoing process of analyzing themes and patterns, with a goal of producing a complete and detailed description of the topic.

The study that piques your interest is on "improvers" and "deteriorators" in group therapy. Hoffmann, Gleave, Burlingame, and Jackson (2009) conducted a qualitative analysis of two groups at a college counseling center, with a focus on empathically understanding the meaning from the participants' perspectives. This use of empathy to understand meaning appeals to you and fits with your philosophies about the best way to study groups. The two groups analyzed were a mixed-gender general therapy group and a group of female sexual assault survivors (Hoffmann et al., 2009). Both groups were co-led by a psychologist and a graduate student trainee. They used the full-scale Outcome Questionnaire-45 (OQ-45; Lambert et al., 1996), with a change score of at least 14 points as their cutoff to determine improvers and deteriorators in the groups.

One of Hoffmann et al.'s (2009) findings initially surprises you. They found that those members who were deteriorators (according to the OQ-45) actually looked like improvers after the reviewer watched the tape. *This finding supports your growing belief that intuition and clinical knowledge is important but that balancing that with objective measures of outcome and change is also needed, especially given the complexities of group therapy.* After several levels of analysis, where the reviewer knew who were improvers and who were deteriorators, six themes emerged from the deteriorators (Hoffmann et al., 2009):

1. In the first sessions of the group, deteriorators had more substantial disclosures, were more open, and spoke more at length.

2. Deteriorators openly praised the process of the group.

3. Deteriorators had an expectation that sharing deep and personal information was required.

4. Deteriorators spent more time giving feedback, especially challenging and confronting others versus working on their own concerns. In this way, they shared less in the group and appeared more as "junior co-leaders."

5. In terms of their relational focus, when they did share, deteriorators struggled the most with family-of-origin issues.

6. The leaders were less likely to process deteriorators' group interactions. Thus, they were almost used more as examples in group than as active members.

Overall, Hoffmann et al. (2009) pointed out that deteriorators openly stated the value of the group but became more wary of participating as the group progressed. Their early enthusiasm for openly sharing in the group may have gotten in the way of leaders seeing them as deteriorators, thus potentially leading them not to challenge their interpersonal patterns that were being enacted in the group (Hoffmann et al., 2009).

There were five themes that emerged for the improvers:

1. Improvers were hesitant and openly cautious of the group process at the beginning of the group.

2. Improvers initiated taking the time for their own work in the group (or took it when it was offered to them).

3. Improvers discussed and accepted credit for their positive life changes.

4. Improvers were mainly concerned about peer relationships and pointed out how their own interactions could change in them.

5. Improvers were actively engaged with by others; for instance, other members checked in with them.

Their findings support others' (e.g., Korda & Pancrazio, 1989) finding that too much self-disclosure too soon can be detrimental to group members.

However, you wonder if there were pregroup differences in the interpersonal styles of the members who were deteriorators versus those who were improvers that led to these different trajectories in group. Despite this question, you find this to be a fascinating study that you'll keep in mind, not to pull causal conclusions from but to use as a reminder for discussing perceptions of group members' progress or deterioration in your case consultations with staff.

Summary

After you finish your reading, you sit back and reflect on your conclusions. Fundamentally, you know that group interventions are effective. You have learned about their effectiveness across a variety of populations, ages, settings, and with varying interventions and theories. The outcomes used to evaluate this effectiveness include measures such as goal attainment, recidivism rates, improvements in social roles, symptom reduction, reduced violence and bullying, and improved interpersonal relationships. This leaves you feeling confident that your new group work program will be an appropriate way to address a variety of college students' needs.

You return to the list of concerns that you heard from your colleagues. You now have ways to address their worries. You decide to create a "Myths and Fears About Group Work" handout that you can use in your training. This will incorporate the evidence on the effectiveness of groups in a way that targets these concerns and other myths about group work that you have heard.

Myths and Fears About Group Work

"I won't improve in group. I might as well just keep doing what I'm doing."

You might be surprised to learn that the average group client is better off than 72% of the controls who were untreated (Burlingame et al., 2003).

"I've been struggling with depression and anxiety for so long. Can a semester-long group even help me?"

In examining group members' scores of depression and anxiety from before their group to after their group, researchers found that both depression and anxiety were significantly reduced due to the group treatment. This review was based on an analysis of 111 studies (Burlingame et al., 2003).

(Continued)

(Continued)

"I don't think being in a co-ed group is for me."

While you may have some specific reasons not to be in a co-ed group, which you should talk to your counselor about, several studies have demonstrated that members in mixed groups do better than those in single-gender groups (Burlingame et al., 2003; Kipper & Ritchie, 2003).

"Being in a group with other people who are depressed can't help me."

While you may think that being around other members who are depressed won't help you change, in fact, research has shown that members who are in groups with others who have similar problems actually improve more than clients in groups with many different problems. You'll likely find that being around others who can really understand what you mean and offer you their own support can be very beneficial.

"What's the point of being in a group with other students? Isn't the advice from the therapist what I need to change?"

In fact, building relationships between members is one of the most helpful aspects of group counseling. It has been proposed that group workers can contribute the most to a group by helping build relationships between the members (Burlingame et al., 2003). Thus, it's not the therapist's advice that is most helpful but his or her ability to help the group develop the most effectively, which includes building relationships between members.

"Won't some of the same issues of discrimination that I've been experiencing in class happen in group?"

Group workers are ethically and morally obligated to help address issues of oppression and marginalization. This also means that they need to help address issues of privilege. Group can be a safe place for members to work on understanding how they might be contributing to ongoing issues of oppression and how they can work to change this. It can also provide others who have been victims with a safe place to heal.

"I don't know if I'm ready for group counseling."

It is important to be honest about this with yourself and your counselor. We know that people who have more positive expectations for group therapy often do better (MacNair-Semands, 2002). Try to think about some of your fears and hesitations, and bring them up with your group worker when you meet before the group starts, or in the early sessions of group.

"Won't having 10 people in a room mean it will just get out of control?"

It is the group workers' responsibility to establish boundaries in the group, set rules, and work with members to help set the norms on how to participate.

_____ **Learning Exercise**

Instructions: Circle whether each statement below is true (T) or false (F).

1. T F It is generally inaccurate to state that some mental health staff continue to possess fears and concerns about group.

2. T F Group treatment generally does at least as well as no treatment or individual treatment.

3. T F Members in single-gender groups tend to do better than those in mixed-gender groups.

4. T F Outpatient groups, homogeneous groups, and groups with a behavioral orientation are associated with greater client improvement.

5. T F A key component to creating a strong group program is to be able to highlight the effectiveness of groups.

6. T F When delivering group work, clinical intuition can be disregarded when objective measures of outcome and change are available.

7. T F High self-disclosure by group members early in a group can be harmful.

8. T F Generally speaking, it is important for group leaders to translate in their practice knowledge about what works with groups.

9. T F The competence of group leaders does not seem to matter if they are drawing from evidence-based practices.

10. T F While it is now assumed that group approaches can be as effective as others, there really is no research evidence to back up that belief.

3 Best Practice Guidelines in Group Work

For all group work, regardless of its type, best practices need to be followed. You decide to use the Association for Specialists in Group Work (ASGW) *Best Practice Guidelines 2007 Revisions* (Thomas & Pender, 2008) as your starting point. You learn that ASGW divides the guidelines into three areas: planning, performing, and processing. Intuitively, this makes sense, and you continue reading and generalizing the guidelines to your practice setting.

Best Practices in Planning

Planning a group is often one of the areas not given enough attention in practice. It can seem that there isn't enough time before the group needs to start meeting the demands of the agency or center. Yet without appropriate preparation, a new group—and indeed a new group work program—can fall apart. Just as pregroup preparation is key for group members (Burlingame et al., 2002; MacKenzie, 2001; Yalom, 2005), so, too, is planning crucial for group leaders.

Best Practice Planning Guideline A1: Follow Professional Practice Components and Codes of Ethics

You see how crucial it is for group workers to know and utilize professional standards (such as the ASGW *Professional Standards for the Training of Group Workers*, ASGW *Best Practice Guidelines*, Association for Multicultural Counseling and Development *Multicultural Counseling Competencies and Standards*). You download and review these documents, consulting with staff when you want to discuss one of them. You recognize that other professions have other group standards and best practice documents (e.g., American Group Psychotherapy Association [AGPA] *Practice*

Guidelines for Group Psychotherapy), and you compile a master list of all these resources for your staff. Because you do not bill insurance at the counseling center, you don't need to investigate the regulations for that, but you make note of a HIPAA (Health Insurance Portability and Accountability Act) course available online if you need one in the future. This guideline also applies to understanding and following professional licensure and certification regulations, so you add information about the National Board for Certified Counselors' requirements to your master list of resources.

Best Practice Planning Guideline A2: Define Your Scope of Practice and Build Your Conceptual Framework

As you have been preparing for the group work coordinator role, you have already been reflecting on your strengths and weaknesses as a group worker, but you decide to formalize it given this guideline. With your individual specialization in mindfulness and stress management, you feel comfortable leading psychoeducational groups on this topic. You are thinking about coleading a group for individuals with eating disorders with a fellow staff member who has more experience with counseling groups and this population. Based on this, you start defining your scope of practice and outlining areas where you want to receive more training. As you get closer to running the groups, you start outlining the proposed content for the mindfulness clinic you have decided to run. This clinic is a four-session group that you'll offer three times per semester at the counseling center. In addition to the content in the outline, you also include group goals and techniques you'll be attending to in each session.

Best Practice Planning Guideline A3: Assess Yourself and Others Through an Ecological Assessment

You have already begun analyzing your attitudes, thoughts, and practices related to beliefs about the change process in groups. You expand this to include how past experiences with any type of group influence you. Groups could include an individual's first group, such as family; experiences with organized teams, clubs, or church groups; and peer and colleague group interactions. As you reflect on these past group experiences, you ask yourself, "What explicit and implicit norms about leader's roles did I learn?" "What members were more powerful or influential, and why?" "What role did I take in these groups?" "How did I react to conflict in these groups?" "How did some of these group experiences mirror inequities and injustices from larger societal issues, such as racism, sexism, homophobia, and so on?" Research has demonstrated that group leaders who are fearful of being members of a group, likely based on past experiences with groups, believe clients are more fearful as well (Marmarosh & Van Horn, 2012).

You wonder how you or any of your staff might avoid affective topics that members may be ready to handle, because of the group worker's own anxieties. Thus, you realize that reflecting on one's own past experiences and how they influence expectations of leader and member experiences is crucial.

Best Practice Planning Guideline A4: Utilize Program Development and Evaluation Strategies

To help you develop a comprehensive group program, you decide to form a small committee of staff members. You work with them to assess other staff members' interests and skills in leading particular groups and to identify how these will meet the needs of the student population. For the next phase of the program development, you work with each new group leader to help him or her write the purpose and goals of the group, which indicate the expected roles group members will play in informing the group goals. You work with the committee to determine that the no-show fee will remain the same as it is for individual counseling. You are sure to include this in your informed consent. You also start planning with the committee how you are going to evaluate groups and consider several group process and outcome measures from the CORE Battery–Revised (Burlingame et al., 2006), as well as several more recent ones, such as the Group Questionnaire (Krogel, 2009). The committee also recommends that once the groups start, there should be a group case consultation for the coleaders, with video review, every other week to ensure that appropriate group techniques and leadership styles are being used. As group work coordinator, you decide to show a recording of your group the first week to help set the norms for what is presented and how fellow staff can be most useful in this consultation.

Best Practice Planning Guideline A5: Identify Resources for Managing the Group Program

You work with your director to ensure the following resources are in place: private and comfortable group rooms; support for coleadership; a marketing strategy to use the college newspaper, Facebook posts, and digital signage to advertise your new group program and specific groups; and support and buy-in from potential referral sources around campus.

Best Practice Planning Guideline A6: Write a Professional Disclosure Statement

You decide to develop a template that your fellow staff members can use to write their professional disclosure statement for each group they are leading. You provide yours as a model for them when you hand out the template.

Your template includes sections for confidentiality and exceptions to confidentiality; group leader's theoretical orientation; information on the purpose and goals of the group; responsibilities of group members; leaders' qualifications for each group; licenses, certifications, and professional affiliations; and information on the licensing or credentialing body (Thomas & Pender, 2008).

Best Practice Planning Guideline A7: Prepare the Members for Group

Knowing that pregroup preparation is key to group members' success in group, you work with the committee to develop a list that you can give to fellow staff. You decide that pregroup preparation should include setting treatment expectations, the anticipated group procedures, role preparation, skill building, and starting the process of setting group norms (Burlingame, Fuhriman, & Johnson, 2001). As you are planning this, you learn that effective pregroup preparation reduces client anxiety, helps align the group worker and members on the goals and tasks of group, and enhances the therapeutic alliance (AGPA, 2007). In addition, you realize that culturally skilled counselors help educate clients in the process of group counseling (Arredondo et al., 1996) as part of the pregroup preparation. Early in group, including a pregroup meeting, is when you want to establish the value of cultural differences as the norm in your groups (Singh, Merchant, Skudrzyk, & Ingene, 2012). When working individually with members of a group prior to the group starting, you want your colleagues to consider specific issues of each member and how those issues will influence their participation in group process and emotional regulation in the group (Marmarosh & Van Horn, 2012).

Best Practice Planning Guideline A8: Engage in Professional Development

In preparation for the increased utilization of groups at your center, you engage in numerous professional development opportunities and offer listings of them to your staff. This includes attending annual and semiannual conferences hosted by the major group organizations, reading professional journals, and attending online teleconferences offered by the group organizations. You follow the guideline regarding seeking supervision or consultation when ethical concerns arise that might interfere with effective functioning; so you make it clear to staff that you are available for consultation and seek out a member within ASGW that you can consult with as necessary.

Best Practice Planning Guideline A9: Be Aware of Environmental and Technological Changes

You subscribe to the American Counseling Association's (ACA) government relations listserv (information available at www.counseling.org/

aca-community/listservs) so you can stay up to date on changes to regula-tions and industry standards. When you attend conferences, you pay special attention to the presentations on technology and growing uses of technological aids (e.g., online groups and marketing through Facebook) in group work. Looking for examples, you come across one that seems especially helpful, as it relates to clinicians who are using social media in their work (see http://drkkolmes.com/for-clinicians/articles/).

_____ **Learning Exercise**

Consider Your Scope of Practice and Conceptual Framework

Best Practice Planning Guideline A2 calls for group workers to define their scope of practice and base their practice on a conceptual framework. Let's pick up with how you intend to focus the scope of your practice around mindfulness and stress management.

The basic question is this:

What is the conceptual framework for group work with a mindfulness and stress management emphasis?

Step 1: We get you started by suggesting one possible component:

Component	**Three Key Concepts**
Positive psychology	Happiness, strengths, resilience

Step 2: Now, it's your turn:

Add two additional components to define a scope of group work practice around mindfulness and stress management; list three key concepts for each component. Feel free to access resources to accomplish this task.

Component	**Three Key Concepts**
1. _____	_____
2. _____	_____

Step 3: Putting it together:

Describe how these components and key concepts connect with group work.

_____

_____

_____

_____.

Best Practices in Performing

These guidelines focusing on group practice highlight the need for aware-ness, flexibility, knowledge of change mechanisms, diversity competence, and appropriate conduct for competent and ethical practice (Thomas & Pender, 2008). You smile as you recall how overwhelmed you were in graduate school when you started leading your first experiential group in the "groups" class. It seemed that there were so many factors to pay attention to that you were overwhelmed. Now as you go through the best practice guidelines, you start seeing the whole picture—in a way, seeing the forest instead of just a multitude of trees.

Best Practice Performing Guideline B1: Develop Self-Knowledge

Self-awareness of cultural heritage (Arredondo et al., 1996) is a key part of planning a group. You know that culturally skilled counselors examine their own emotional reactions toward other cultural groups (Arredondo et al., 1996) so they do not prove detrimental in the performing and processing phases of group leadership. You believe that until you have embarked on the process to explore your own cultural heritage, making use of contextual fac-tors to understand others' experiences is only half the process. You value recognizing your own biases and assumptions and know that it assists you in identifying how group members' cultural context influences them. As you think about this further, you wonder how a cultural context influences indi-viduals in their definition of the problem, communication styles in group, avoidance of certain topics in group, or in the impact of political and eco-nomic realities that oppress communities and, in turn, individual members in group. You make a mental note of this to bring up at the next committee meeting for a larger group discussion.

Best Practice Performing Guideline B2: Perform Core and Unique Group Competencies

You review the ASGW *Professional Standards for the Training of Group Workers* (Wilson, Rapin, & Haley-Banez, 2000) to ground yourself in the core group competencies. You start thinking of what some unique group competencies might be. From your reading, you know that providing higher levels of structure early in group helps reduce anxiety, which in turn may lead to greater disclosures and higher levels of cohesion (Burlingame et al., 2001). This structure is especially useful in counseling and psychotherapy groups but also in psychoeducational groups, where member-to-member interactions are also encouraged. Although counseling and psy-chotherapy groups typically employ less-structured techniques than do task and psychoeducational groups, they can still be quite useful. For example, you really like how Johnson (2009) provided ways to use early group structure (e.g., introductory exercises, encouraging thinking and feeling out loud) for interpersonal process groups in college counseling centers, and you want to follow this model for the "Understanding Self and Others" groups that your center will offer.

Best Practice Performing Guideline B3: Be Open to Adapting Your Group

You know it is critical to be flexible when working with groups. This includes being able to modify your techniques to be appropriate to the group type and stage, as well as to the needs of the group members (Thomas & Pender, 2008). For some groups, this may mean group workers modeling norms and interpersonal behaviors that increase member-to-member interactions (Burlingame et al., 2001; Wilson et al., 2000). Leaders can model appropriate disclosures, particularly those related to here-and-now reactions to group process, which are often difficult for new group members to identify and initiate. Burlingame et al. (2001) proposed that group workers can contribute the most to a group by building relationships between members. This leads to the creation of the social microcosm, in which members' interpersonal dynamics are re-created inside the group and do not need to be relayed through history taking or storytelling (Yalom, 2005). Group workers need to monitor how group members progress toward their goals, and adjust as appropriate to ensure that the group moves toward them. Finally, this guideline also dictates that group leaders maintain appropriate boundaries with group members, which may look different depending on the type of group, location, and their role in the organization.

Best Practice Performing Guideline B4: Implement Effective Use of Therapeutic Conditions and Dynamics

Group workers need to be able to adjust the pace of the group based on the group's stage of development (Wilson et al., 2000). For example, early in group in the forming stage, leaders may work toward more horizontal disclosures from members, thus fostering more opportunities for universality and identification of similarities between members. Later in group—for instance, in the norming and performing stages—group workers should encourage more vertical disclosures when there is sufficient safety and cohesion to support this kind of disclosure. Other member behaviors that should be encouraged include turn taking (although not in a rote, one-by-one method), nonjudgmental emotional responses, and the encouragement of emotional expression (Marmarosh & Van Horn, 2012). You know that the power of groups can also be detrimental (e.g., if members feel forced to self-disclose before they are ready due to peer pressure), and this guideline puts the responsibility of protecting group members on the group worker.

Best Practice Performing Guideline B5: Assist in Meaning Attribution

Group workers need to attend to the cognitive processing that members do to make sense of their group experiences. As Yalom (2005) proposed, group work includes an emotional experience as well as a cognitive understanding. An exclusive focus on either one is detrimental.

Best Practice Performing Guideline B6: Work Collaboratively With Group Members

As you have been reading, it is clear to you that group members need to play a key role in setting their goals and cocreating the group experience. In this way, the group leader is more of a facilitator of group process, rather than the leader who dictates exactly what direction it is going to go in.

Best Practice Performing Guideline B7: Evaluate Your Work

You work with your committee to develop an evaluation form that you'll use at the end of each semester with your group members. You want to get their perspectives, both numerical ratings using a Likert-type scale and open-ended responses, to get their evaluation of the group. You also start discussing with the committee if staff should use process measures (available in the CORE-R Battery; Burlingame et al., 2006) as a way to evaluate groups between sessions to evaluate progress.

Best Practice Performing Guideline B8: Embrace Diversity

You strongly believe that group leaders should address issues of privilege and oppression in their groups (Singh et al., 2012). It often becomes your role as a group leader to highlight topics that might be typically taboo in general conversations to help a group start exploring them (Johnson, Torres, Coleman, & Smith, 1995). You realize how this process is made easier if the potential for these conversations is brought up at the pregroup meeting or in the first few sessions of a group, and you add this to your pregroup preparation checklist for fellow staff members.

You know it might be hard for staff to address this, so you provide some examples, such as what it might be like for them to address issues of racial microaggressions. In this way, they could provide some examples and education around microaggressions to help members understand the subtle nature of many of these interactions, in addition to engaging the members in processing what this type of discussion would be like. When groups are ready to engage in such discussions, your staff can use structured exercises and questions to help discussions. Burnes and Ross (2010) provided useful questions such as, "How do you think we often marginalize each other in our space today?" and "Why do you believe this person has power?" to help the group focus on here-and-now interactions rather than highlighting instances of oppression outside of group. In this way, you'll address cultural conflicts (Singh et al., 2012), thus working not to perpetuate societal injustices in your groups.

Best Practice Performing Guideline B9: Maintain Awareness of Ethical Considerations

You are careful not to get isolated in your thinking about groups, bringing ethical concerns and questions up to fellow staff or your mentor from ASGW. You follow ethical standards from ACA and ASGW and try to highlight ethical considerations when having discussions with colleagues.

Learning Exercise

Apply Therapeutic Conditions and Dynamics

As you've read, one of the important therapeutic dynamics is *group development*. Most models indicate that the early sessions of any group require attention to helping members become oriented to the task at hand, whether that be personal growth or goal accomplishment, and helping them become a part of the group as it evolves.

How can group workers assist in these goals?

Follow these steps:

1. Form a new group of five to nine people.

2. Select a facilitator.

3. For 20 minutes, discuss the topic: Agree on *three key ways* group workers can help a group and its members positively move through the early sessions.

4. Hold a 10-minute review session responding to the two questions:

   a. How were you feeling during the discussion?

   b. How effectively did you all work to help yourselves and others become oriented and included?

Best Practices in Processing

As you think about the importance of processing group work, you remember how valuable supervision was for you as a trainee. It was in the processing of the experiences that you really learned from them—not just the actual group interactions themselves but the meaning and lessons you took away from them. You make a silent commitment to yourself not to get too busy for processing and to prioritize it for your trainees and fellow colleagues.

Best Practice Processing
Guideline C1: Prioritize Processing

You work with your group committee, as well as consulting with your director, to schedule time for processing and supervision with trainees for the group work. This means scheduling specific times when group workers assess members' progress, their own leadership, and whole-group dynamics. You decide that for most of the co-led groups, group workers will have 30 minutes of supervision both before and after their 90-minute groups.

Best Practice Processing
Guideline C2: Develop a Reflective Practice

Developing a reflective practice takes time. It requires effort to synthesize theory into practice, but you make a commitment to continue reading and expanding your theoretical knowledge about groups even after this initial planning phase for the group work program. Creating a reflective practice means that leaders should process the member-to-member interactions in the group. This includes hypothesizing about behaviors between members in a group (Wilson et al., 2000), yet you want to be careful not to pathologize specific ways of relating (Burnes & Ross, 2010). One way you want to be on the lookout for this is in examining the role of silence and how it might be a member's way of coping with oppression (Burnes & Ross, 2010), rather than an interpersonal deficit. This kind of processing does not need to happen just before or after a group but can also happen during a group. Highlighting instances of oppression or exploring unintentional microaggressions can be most effective in the moment (Burnes & Ross, 2010). You can also help members identify and explore the external barriers (e.g., systemic patterns of oppression and privilege) that impact their growth and development (Lewis, Arnold, House, & Toporek, 2003).

Best Practice Processing Guideline C3: Use Formative and Summative Evaluations

Group workers need to evaluate the process and outcomes of groups. As Chapman and colleagues (2012) found, group therapists underestimate the number of clients who deteriorate in group and do not accurately perceive the group members' perceptions of the group relationship. Thus, the need for using process and outcome measures in group is clear.

Best Practice Processing Guideline C4: Consult With and Train Others When Appropriate

When processing group experiences after the group, you know it is tempting for beginning group leaders to focus only on the member-to-member and member-to-leader experiences. However, leader attention also needs to be paid to the group as a whole (Burlingame et al., 2001). You decide to put together a brief training on processing at the macro level. This entails examining "how the group is functioning" and exploring "the collection of individual members' unconscious wishes, fears, fantasies, and needs" (Brown, 2003, p. 233). Brown provides questions that can be asked to process this macro level of group experiences, and you present these to your staff:

What is the group doing to promote safety?

How is the group establishing norms, and what norms are in place and/ or emerging?

What is the group's reaction to authority?

What is threatening the group?

How does the group manage conflict, anxiety, arousal, and other uncomfortable states?

What is the group's reaction to anticipated intimacy?

What significant and important feelings are expressed or ignored?

How is the group managing its work or task?

What is the prevailing theme of the group at this time?

What personal feelings and reactions am I experiencing? Are these from the group, or are they in response to my unresolved issues?

Does the group seem stuck? (p. 234)

Within this group-as-a-whole level of processing, you work with your staff to assess communication and interpersonal patterns with regard to their cultural relevance and appropriateness (Johnson et al., 1995). In this way, you are embodying the best practice guideline (Thomas & Pender, 2008) to consult and train with others when appropriate.

Learning Exercise _____

Scheduling Processing

You've read (see Best Practice Processing Guideline C1) about the importance of processing and the need to include it within group sessions and, for the leader or coleaders, to build it into a regular meeting schedule outside of the group.

Context for This Learning Exercise

Imagine you are coleading a stress-management group. During its planning, the two of you discussed the importance of establishing a weekly meeting time to process your experience as coleaders. However, it seems to you there has been some slippage. One week your coleader cancelled apologetically due to an emergency, and then the following week he was 20 minutes late. As you've thought about this, you've become concerned and wonder if you should bring your concerns up with your coleader.

Step 1: (5 minutes) Individually consider this situation. Identify *one issue* that seems to be at stake.

Step 2: (5 minutes) Develop *two ways* to address the issue. For instance, if an issue might be your own reluctance to initiate discussion with your coleader, generate two ways you might work this through positively.

Step 3: Pair up with another.

Step 4: Role-play leader and coleader in the situation described.

   a. First, in Round 1 (you as leader), work with the issue you identified and try out each way you identified (5 minutes each way).

   b. Second, in Round 2 (you as coleader), your partner works with the issue he or she identified and then tries out each way identified (5 minutes each way).

Step 5: Process your learning (10 minutes). What did you learn? What might you be able to apply?

_____

_____

_____

_____

_____.

Summary

As you finish reviewing the *Best Practice Guidelines* (Thomas & Pender, 2008), you notice an inner sense of calm. You realize this comes from the feeling of security you are experiencing. Knowing how much effort and time others have put into creating these guidelines, with all the experience and research that went into them, assures you. You know you have a strong basis for your decisions and are building the group work program on a solid foundation.

4 Multicultural Competency and Social Justice in Group Work

You know that groups—if they are safe for members—can be a place for members to talk about topics they do not discuss outside of group. These discussions can include interpersonal feedback that is considered "taboo" in other social settings or intergroup dialogue discussions helping build awareness and understanding of others. Yet you also know that some of the hardest topics to explore in group include issues of discrimination, oppression, and privilege. Often group leaders can feel underequipped to guide these discussions and interactions in ways that are therapeutic and not harmful to the group members. You decide to investigate some of the key issues and build a cognitive framework for multicultural competency and social justice advocacy in groups.

You consult the Association for Specialists in Group Work *Multicultural and Social Justice Competence Principles for Group Workers* (Singh, Merchant, Skudrzyk, & Ingene, 2012) and are reminded that group workers are ethically and morally obligated to address issues of oppression and marginalization; this requirement means that they also address issues of privilege (Burnes & Ross, 2010; Singh et al., 2012). As you think further about this, more than just being an obligation, attention to social justice, multicultural understanding, and empowerment can be rewarding, health producing, and inspiring.

For group workers and members to strive toward social justice and empowerment takes courage, skill, and dedication. In this process, you plan to engage with your colleagues in a "process of self-reflection, learning, and action," which is termed "taking action" (Singh et al., 2012, p. 3). This is an active process—not an end result—in which "group workers move towards multicultural and social justice advocacy competence" (p. 3). You are excited by this intention but also a bit daunted as you think about how you can work to create an inclusive and empowered group environment (Ratts, Anthony, & Santos, 2010) that promotes social justice (Burnes & Ross, 2010).

You come across several key terms throughout your reading:

Diversity: "Different types of people in a group or society" (Singh et al., 2012, p. 1).

Multicultural: "The belief systems and typical daily activities of people from various diverse groups, and denotes that attending to the needs and values of these diverse groups ensures a more vibrant, dynamic, and empowered society overall" (Singh et al., 2012, p. 2). Multiculturalism includes three components: recognizing an individual's unique worldview, appreciating sociocultural differences, and working toward empowerment of others (Singh et al., 2012).

Social justice: "The awareness of how social locations of social privilege and oppression influence group work processes and dynamics" (Singh et al., 2012, p. 2) with a goal to "ensure that every individual has an equal opportunity to be a contributing member of society and have access to quality resources such as education, healthcare, and employment" (Ratts et al., 2010, p. 161).

Social privilege: "Power and advantage a dominant group is granted, entitled to, or born into" (Singh et al., 2012, p. 2).

Intrapersonal Awareness

You're aware that one of the first steps toward social justice is for a group worker to focus on him or herself. Group workers should strive to develop an awareness of their own identity that is based on their experiences and histories with privilege and oppression (Singh et al., 2012). You recall the structured activities and discussions you had in your classes, such as through genealogical interviews, spiritual history exercises, and reflections on group supervision. But since you graduated, you haven't had opportunities to participate in such guided experiences. You believe it's crucial for this to continue throughout one's career and not just in the process of formal schooling; therefore, you decide to collect some resources for your own development and decide to offer them to your colleagues as well. You gather books such as *White Like Me: Reflections on Race From a Privileged Son* (Wise, 2011), *Hombres y Machos: Masculinity and Latino Culture* (Mirandé, 1997), and *Gardens in the Dunes* (Silko, 2000), and videos such as *The Color of Fear* (Lee, Hunter, Goss, & Bock, 1997). You also make a note to seek out professional development opportunities focusing on social justice. You consult DeLucia-Waack and Donigian (2004) for a list of resources, including books and chapters, popular movies, journal articles, and videos relevant to multicultural counseling. Through this process of building awareness, you want to help group workers understand their own cultural context and hypothesize how their norms and values influence the counseling process (Johnson, Torres, Coleman, & Smith, 1995).

You begin reflecting on your Western, middle-class values (note: we develop this example around a group worker from a White, European background) and how they play out in the norms and expectations you hold. For instance, the expectations of having a goal of self-development, not giving advice, and opening up to strangers about personal issues are topics you start reflecting on as being culturally embedded in your values. You wonder how your own cultural heritage influences your beliefs about "normal" and "abnormal" development (Arredondo et al., 1996). For instance, continuing to subconsciously hold on to a lingering family-of-origin belief that "we are independent, we can handle our own business, thank you very much, and need no one to rush to our help" would seem to conflict with the basic helping assumption underlying group work itself.

You read that culturally skilled White counselors should identify how they have benefited from social privilege and institutional racism, both in their present lives and in their families' pasts (Arredondo et al., 1996). Working to build this self-awareness is critical, as the extent to which social justice is incorporated depends on a counselor's expertise, comfort, and familiarity in dealing with issues of privilege and oppression (Ratts et al., 2010).

Learning Exercise

Intrapersonal Awareness: Who Am I?

1. What do you know about yourself? Answer the following questions:

   What is your . . .

   - chronological age and developmental stage?
   - gender?
   - race?
   - ethnicity?
   - socioeconomic situation?
   - family history?
   - geographic location?
   - physical health?
   - psychological maturity?
   - worldview?
   - level of social support?
   - political orientation?
   - spiritual/religious involvement?
   - belief about how change occurs?
   - comfort level with yourself?

   What do you . . .

   - value?
   - find meaningful?

What are your . . .

- work interests?
- avocational interests?

How do you now or intend to . . .

- define the helper role?
- apply the helper role?
- take care of yourself?
- take care of others?

2. Reflect on your answers to the above questions. What meaning is there for you as a group work leader?

3. Discuss your thoughts with a partner (15 minutes per person).

Interpersonal Factors

Culturally skilled group workers strive to become knowledgeable about the families, values, and communities where their group members live (Arredondo et al., 1996). You realize that through this knowledge, combined with your own self-awareness, you would be better able to identify and address differences in communication styles between group members and/or leaders (Singh et al., 2012). As you ponder this thought, your reading assists you in identifying one example of it: the differences between high-context and low-context communication styles (Singh et al., 2012). With high-context communication, the speaker typically uses fewer words and lets the cultural context help explain. In contrast, with low-context communication, the speaker is more explicit. If some of your group members come from a background where a high-context communication style is the norm, they could assume that an individual who has a low-context communication style is rambling or adding irrelevant details or facts. They may then assume that the member has communication and interpersonal problems that need to be addressed through the group. However, this perspective privileges the high-context method of communicating and does not value the diversity present in the group.

You have learned that culturally competent group workers not only attend to interpersonal differences in their groups but also to how larger systems, such as sociopolitical and economic forces, influence group members (Ratts et al., 2010). This broadened level of awareness includes exploring issues such as immigration and poverty (Arredondo et al., 1996)—for instance, understanding how lack of health care access can affect the well-being of a group member. You recall other work you have done on behalf of individual clients, such as advocacy at the county level for increased coverage for residents with no mental health insurance coverage. You realize that you could also do this work on behalf of group clients, perhaps even including them in the decision-making process of what advocacy work you and the counseling center will do.

You realize the necessity to avoid a color-blind norm in groups, where all cultural differences are explicitly ignored, because it carries the consequence of denying the reality of someone's experience (Johnson et al., 1995). When working with members who are bilingual, you know you should strive to actively value bilingualism (Singh et al., 2012) and not view a client's language as a barrier to counseling (Arredondo et al., 1996). You recall a video clip on group interaction (Corey, Corey, & Haynes, 2006), in which the group leaders encourage a woman to speak in her native language to give feedback to each group member. This allows her to interact in a very different way with the group members and thus provides a source of interpersonal reflection in the group. The empowerment that she feels and the impact on the other members are addressed in the video. You make a note to include this in your list of resources for staff, and perhaps will even show it during some of the orientation trainings you conduct.

Your review also stresses the importance of group workers' attending to intracultural differences of members to avoid labeling and stereotyping members from a similar culture (Singh et al., 2012). When this occurs, group members are not treated as if they all have the same cultural experiences, whether they share a common identity or not. Attending to multiple and multilayered identities of group members also is good practice for group leaders (Singh et al., 2012). For instance, in some circumstances, an African American male member may be informed more by his racial identity and Christian beliefs. Yet, in discussing other areas of his life, such as his academics in an engineering department, he may be more influenced by being a gay man and struggling with homophobia among his colleagues. When this group member is disclosing about his experiences in his department and sharing examples of some of the interpersonal behaviors he has experienced, you know it will be important for the group worker to question whether he is responding to bias and homophobia or has a pervasive suspicion of others in his department.

Ridley's (2005) typology seems useful to keep in mind in working to understand this client's experiences. Ridley described the differences between cultural paranoia, "a minority group member's healthy reaction to racism," and functional paranoia, "an unhealthy psychological condition" (p. 64), and how these interact with the member's self-disclosure to counselors of various racial backgrounds. Ridley considered a "healthy cultural paranoiac" to be a client who has high levels of cultural paranoia and low levels of functional paranoia and who is more likely to disclose to an ethnic minority therapist than to a White therapist. An "intercultural nonparanoiac discloser" is low on both cultural and functional paranoia and will likely disclose to either an ethnic minority counselor or a White counselor. Thus, it is crucial not only for the group leader to assess how the member is functioning but also to assess the member's levels of self-disclosure in relation to the group leader's characteristics. The focus is interpersonal and interactional in nature, not just an intrapsychic exploration of the group member.

Another interactional process to be aware of in groups is whether the group is replicating dominant-minority relations that may be oppressive inside the group (Eason, 2009). The following questions, adapted from Conyne (1989), can aid in this process:

- Are members resentful that they have to understand others?
- Do some members act as though their ideas are similar?
- Do members from minority identities/cultures make suggestions for the best way to proceed?
- Which topics does the group spend time on? Are these related to cultural background?
- Are certain topics, such as racism, avoided in the group?
- How do the group norms relate to current societal issues, such as empowerment, oppression, and so on?
- Are subgroups based on cultural identity?
- What are the levels of verbal participation? Who talks to whom?
- What are the levels of influence between members?
- Do members hesitate to discuss their unique cultural concerns?

Learning Exercise

Identifying Culturally Relevant Group Processes

The purpose of this exercise is to apply interpersonal awareness within a small group.

Step 1: Form a small group, preferably one that contains some noticeable forms of diversity (e.g., age, gender, race, ethnicity).

Step 2: Choose a multicultural topic to discuss in a 30-minute time period. Suggested topics: "challenges faced by gay, lesbian, and transsexual people in today's society"; "ways counselors can increase their competency to work with senior citizens"; "how attitudes and values affect our interactions with people who are different from us."

Step 3: Select a group facilitator to guide the 30-minute topical discussion.

Step 4: Following the discussion, spend 15 minutes discussing group member observations of group processes that occurred. Focus on culturally based processes, such as those mentioned in the section preceding this exercise (Conyne, 1989).

Step 5: Identify and discuss the learning acquired.

Social Justice Advocacy

As discussed earlier, group workers explore and discuss how privilege and oppressive systems influence leaders' and members' lives (Singh et al., 2012), but they also have an opportunity through their group work to take action at the systems level. At a group level, you can strive to increase access to groups for all members of a community, thus working toward equity and equal access to services (Singh et al., 2012). Group workers can partner with target populations to help ensure that the format, location, and concepts of the group fit the cultural context of the group members (Singh et al., 2012). One way that you anticipate doing this is in partnering with some of the other university departments. You have already reached out to the Office of Global Programs for collaborating to meet the needs of a growing international student population. You also want to meet with the staff at the Multicultural Student Resource Center. You know that the needs of some groups may dictate holding them off-site (e.g., at a location at the Multicultural Student Resource Center), cofacilitating with one of their counselors, and having an open group for members who are unsure of what a support group can offer them.

Group workers can help clients negotiate systems, such as access to health care or housing opportunities. When group workers encounter systemic barriers in their work, they develop plans for confronting them (Lewis, Arnold, House, & Toporek, 2003). This could include serving on a local, state, or national committee that is working to take action to address injustices and advocating for access to services and resources.

Social Justice Model

As you think more about social justice and how this can be actualized in your groups, you decide to seek out some more guidance. One of your colleagues gave you an article by Ratts et al. (2010), who provided a conceptual framework with their "Dimensions of Social Justice Model." This is a developmental framework that is influenced by the counselor's comfort and expertise with issues pertaining to social justice.

As you study their model, you discover that *naiveté* is its first dimension. Naiveté is characterized by an intrapsychic and ethnocentric perspective in group, through which cultural variables are not considered. Group leaders in this stage may ignore cultural variables and differences in group members that could account for conflict between them, assuming it is a normal group phase of development (Ratts et al., 2010). As the dimension name implies, if group workers do not see this conflict through a lens that informs them of the cultural dynamics, then they can't process and help the group understand the impact of it. You recall some of your earlier years in graduate school, when you most likely were in this stage. As you look back on some of your teaching experiences, you remember some of the racial tensions and even outright homophobic statements that were made in your class. Even if you noticed them, you didn't know how to address them. This memory brings up a bit of shame, which you notice but try not to judge. It's a reminder of how important it is to continue building your awareness and skills.

The second dimension, *multicultural integration*, is characterized by a group in which leaders and members are trying to understand one another within a cultural context (Ratts et al., 2010). This includes how culture influences their thinking about problems, conflict, and the relationships among members. When a conflict arises, the group leader helps process it in terms of how cultural misunderstandings may have contributed to the conflict (Ratts et al., 2010).

You recall one of your groups where you helped facilitate this kind of conversation. In your group, members were discussing their typical roles in speaking out when they saw a problem, whether in their classes, family relationships, or even an encounter with a stranger at a store. Some of the members who were from the majority racial group for the area (in this case, European American students) seemed to take it for granted that their comments about a problem would be appreciated and encouraged. With further exploration, they were able to see that this was a privilege they had been taking for granted. When listening to an international student from China, they learned that her cultural value of maintaining harmony in a family or group would stop her from speaking out in this way. Group members also considered how their majority race group influenced the reactions they got, compared with the experiences of several members who were Latino American and African American, who explained the kinds of subtle, and at times overt, disrespect they had received when they tried to speak out. Through these kinds of discussions, you hope that group members can develop a deeper appreciation in group for cultural differences and a growing desire to connect positively with those who are in some way unlike them. As group leaders come to realize that awareness and integration of multicultural influences—while important—isn't enough, this propels them toward the third dimension: *liberatory critical consciousness* (Ratts et al., 2010).

This third dimension is characterized by a *cognitive and emotional awakening* (Ratts et al., 2010, p. 164) in which members begin to realize how their lived experiences have deeper "political, social, and historical roots" (p. 164). Through reframing, group leaders can help members begin to externalize the problem and, when appropriate, attribute it to oppressive forces, such as racism, homophobia, sexism, and so forth. In this way, group members no longer view some problems as resulting solely from intrapsychic mechanisms that perpetuate self-blame but, rather, can understand how larger social injustices also may have influenced their beliefs and experiences. You recall hearing some of your colleagues talk about their groups with female graduate students and how the students come to see the unfair structure of the system (e.g., low pay, disrespect toward women in sciences, being tied to the hierarchical system of working for one advisor) in a way that helps shift their sense of the problem's origins.

The fourth dimension, *empowerment*, is built on a foundation that awareness and knowledge are not enough for change. Group members need to find their voices, build on their strengths, and use their self-advocacy skills (Ratts et al., 2010) to help create change at a wider level. This could include partnering with other groups or agencies working to build social justice and develop allies in their fight toward change. You wonder what type of work might be possible in this dimension when doing outreach with the university's Women's Resource Center. You recall some of the statistics on sexual assault on college campuses from the American Association of University Women website (see www.aauw.org/what-we-do/legal-resources/online-resource-library/campus-sexual-assault/). You wonder how an advocacy program can be created to partner with the Women's Resource Center to help provide more resources for survivors of sexual assault. This could include free services at the university health clinic immediately following a sexual assault or working with the local hospital to improve the flow of events if a survivor also wants to press charges. Change could also take place to raise awareness on college campuses with a number of different outreach topics for the general population, such as bringing speakers from the Consensual Project (see www.theconsensualproject.com; focusing on consent "from hookups to relationships") or showing films such as *NO! The Rape Documentary* (Simmons, 2006; see http://notherapedocumentary.org) or *Hip-Hop: Beyond Beats and Rhymes* (Hurt, 2006; resource guide available at www.bhurt.com to facilitate learning and discussions on American pop culture and American manhood as depicted through hip-hop).

The final dimension, *social justice advocacy*, works to take the issue beyond a group by equipping members to advocate with and on behalf of a cause (Ratts et al., 2010). In this dimension, leaders have a responsibility to teach members about changing systems and the steps involved in this process.

This approach is an evolving one in mental health and, more recently, in group work. Decades ago, Conyne and Harding (1976) detailed a general advocacy procedure used by student paraprofessionals of a university counseling center to generate and apply environmental assessment data for advocacy projects. In this approach, these paraprofessionals operated in an ongoing group whose purpose was to discuss and process data that had been systematically collected about campus issues experienced as being generally problematic for students. Guided by a group facilitator, the paraprofessional students (a) identified stressors in the campus environment based on the data, such as feeling unsafe on campus; (b) specified possible personal and environmental causal factors; (c) generated potential change recommendations; and (d) charted concrete action or advocacy plans they or others (the latter frequently being counseling center staff consultants) could take to seek to implement the recommendations. A particular emphasis was placed on environmental causes and solutions. In one outcome of using this advocacy approach, planning produced by the paraprofessional group members was influential in bringing to the attention of campus administrators the need for increased lighting in an especially dark area of the campus that had been the scene of past attacks. Continued advocacy efforts resulted over time in the installation of an expanded lighting system, which contributed to increased safety on campus.

Here was a case of students learning and applying a process for change advocacy in a group that is generalizable to other situations beyond campus safety, such as issues we have been discussing related to the full range of oppressive forces. Other leads for generating advocacy efforts can be found by exploring the advocacy cube developed by Lewis et al. (2003), which includes micro- and macro-level efforts taken with clients or on their behalf, aimed at improvements for individuals, groups, and systems.

Learning Exercise

Promoting Social Justice

The purpose of this exercise is to generate ideas for how to promote social justice in a group.

a. Form a different small group from that used in the previous exercise.

b. Using the Ratts et al. (2010) model as a guide, generate three group-work leader strategies that could be used within each of the five dimensions included.

c. Conclude with a summary discussion. What did you learn?

Dimensions and suggested strategies:

1. Naiveté

Suggested Strategy 1: _____

Suggested Strategy 2: _____

Suggested Strategy 3: _____

2. Multicultural integration

Suggested Strategy 1: _____

Suggested Strategy 2: _____

Suggested Strategy 3: _____

3. Liberatory critical consciousness

Suggested Strategy 1: _____

Suggested Strategy 2: _____

Suggested Strategy 3: _____

4. Empowerment

Suggested Strategy 1: _____

Suggested Strategy 2: _____

Suggested Strategy 3: _____

5. Social justice advocacy

Suggested Strategy 1: _____

Suggested Strategy 2: _____

Suggested Strategy 3: _____

Discuss what you learned through completing this exercise.

Summary

So much to think about, so much to do! Indeed, how does a group leader move toward establishing a positive group climate, using change processes to reach desired goals? What an important question, you realize—one you can't wait to try clarifying.

5

Key Change Processes in Group Work

You're beginning to construct a basic but comprehensive picture of group work through all your study and analysis. A critically important foundation, you conclude, is centered on what leaders of any type of group are seeking to do: "To assist an interdependent collection of people to reach their mutual goals which may be intrapersonal, interpersonal, or work related" (Wilson, Rapin, & Haley-Banez, 2000, p. 3). So simply put, you think, yet it remains a daunting task for you; within the vast array of potential group processes, how can you help navigate the group toward positive therapeutic and productive outcomes? Especially given the four areas of specialization (task group facilitation, group psychoeducation, group counseling, and group psychotherapy), how will you and your colleagues arrive at the intended destination?

This chapter provides a focus on the key change processes in group work. This work has been based largely on person-change groups (therapy, counseling, and psychoeducation). Yet task group leaders can also find value in this information, for they, too, must create cohesive groups where members can connect and work together—not to change personally but to reach productive goals. So let's begin this discussion of change processes by considering task groups.

Task Groups

Leaders of effective task groups are successful in converting a collection of people into a *team* (Cohen & Bailey, 1997). Kormanski (1999) observed that all teams are groups but not all groups are teams. A team needs agreed-on purpose, with the members having developed the capacity to work together in a coordinated way. Moreover, a team is characterized by the adoption of goals to which members are committed, by interdependent functioning among them as they work toward accomplishing those goals, and by accountability toward one another.

51

The group leader's primary role in task groups is to foster the conditions necessary for a sense of "team" to emerge and be sustained as members work toward accomplishing explicit goals. Note that the leader role is *not* to control, direct, or coerce, as it may be typically thought of. The task group leader is much more of a facilitator than a controller (Conyne, 2013).

Developing these conditions, analogous to the therapeutic factors in person-change groups to be discussed below, frees members of a task group to function effectively as active participants in the group and, even more so, as managers of it. Hackman (2011) indicated that member management of a task group accounts for around 60% of the variation in how it will perform. Additional important factors relate to the group leader helping the team get off to a strong start (about 30% of the variance) and then following up with ongoing support and coaching (about 10%).

Drawing from a broader perspective, Schwarz (2002) indicates that effective task groups rely on interactions occurring among group *context* (e.g., supportive culture), *group structure* (e.g., clearly defined roles), and *group process* (e.g., coordination of effort, problem solving). He suggested that these three overall criteria apply for effective task groups: (a) The products delivered meet or exceed performance standards, (b) the processes and structures of the group facilitate its performance, and (c) involvement in the group advances the personal growth and well-being of its members. To these three criteria, Weisbord (1978) would add the importance of leaders keeping everything in balance through attending to building and maintaining positive member relationships, rewarding constructive behaviors, and coordinating productive efforts. Keep these factors in mind as you read next about the five change processes involved in person-change groups; you will no doubt find overlap and consistency.

Sources of Change in Person-Change Groups

Five sources contribute to therapeutic outcomes in person-change (counseling, therapy, psychoeducation) group work (Burlingame, MacKenzie, & Strauss, 2004):

a. Client or member characteristics

b. Leader characteristics

c. Structural factors

d. Formal change theory

e. Small group processes

Burlingame, Strauss, and Joyce (2013) emphasized that it is "up to the group leader, who determines how these sources are integrated, whether the group is used as a vehicle of change or if individual therapy is conducted in a group setting without regard for group dynamic factors" (p. 641). Given the critical role each of these sources plays in contributing to therapeutic outcomes, you decide to investigate each of these areas further to develop information that you and your colleagues might draw from in guiding future groups.

Client/Member Characteristics

Client or member characteristics include both out-of-group characteristics, such as pregroup expectations, and in-group behaviors and characteristics, such as interpersonal style (Burlingame, 2010). One important example of pregroup characteristics is motivational readiness to change. This was found as a key factor for the working alliance in men who were in group counseling for relationship abuse (Taft, Murphy, Musser, & Remington, 2004). Interestingly, MacNair-Semands (2002) found that students at college counseling centers with previous therapy experience had more positive expectations for group. These two studies highlight the importance of assessing expectations, working to modify negative ones, and building motivation for change in pregroup meetings before group members actually start group.

Several factors can help predict attendance and dropout. Within a university counseling center, you noted that two interpersonal styles were found to predict poor attendance (social phobia/inhibition and angry hostility; MacNair-Semands, 2002). Another study found a number of factors that were predictive of premature termination (e.g., dropout) in a day treatment program for individuals with personality disorders: previous hospitalization, younger age, more severe borderline personality disorder traits, and lower previous service utilization (Ogrodniczuk et al., 2008).

This information supplements the large body of literature you find from the Vancouver/Edmonton research project (Ogrodniczuk, Piper, Joyce, McCallum, & Rosie, 2003; Ogrodniczuk, Piper, McCallum, Joyce, & Rosie, 2002; Piper, Ogrodniczuk, Joyce, Weideman, & Rosie, 2007), which explored personality and interpersonal predictors in group psychotherapy for complicated grief. Ogrodniczuk et al. (2003) concluded that "*higher* extraversion, conscientiousness, and openness, and *lower* neuroticism were each associated with more favorable outcome" (p. 432; emphasis in original). Although a different population at your college counseling center, you expect that these personality traits would likely translate as important in your setting as well.

Another factor that has emerged out of this research team's work is quality of object relations (QOR), which is "a person's enduring tendency to establish certain types of relationships that range along an overall dimension from primitive to mature" (Piper et al., 2007, p. 116). Based on their previous work regarding the importance of QOR (e.g., Ogrodniczuk et al., 2002), they focused in their 2007 study on the composition of groups. Specifically, they investigated whether homogeneous, high-QOR groups receiving interpretive group therapy or homogeneous, low-QOR groups receiving supportive group therapy would perform better. You are intrigued to read that neither the individual member's level of QOR nor the form of treatment was the best predictor of outcome; rather, the composition (e.g., percentage of high-QOR clients in each group) was the most important. That is, groups with a higher percentage of clients with a high QOR had better outcomes. This finding highlights the more recent trend in investigating the impact of client characteristics, specifically as they interact with the type of group approach or other group format characteristics (Burlingame et al., 2013). This strikes you as emphasizing the power of the group, rather than any individual's contribution to it, as a key factor to evaluate.

Leader Characteristics

Similar to the client domain, these are characteristics that can be observed both outside of group and in group through specific behaviors. You return to a classic study to start your investigation on leader characteristics, a study that categorized four basic functions of a group leader (Lieberman, Yalom, & Miles, 1973, p. 174). One of these, *caring*, includes how the leader sets the tone of the group and also affection, acceptance, and support. This function contributes to the therapeutic alliance with the group members and conveys positive regard. Fitting with your beliefs, you find that research supports leader characteristics of warmth, empathy, and openness as being related to positive therapeutic outcome (Burlingame & Beecher, 2008).

A more recent study you find provides some more detailed evidence. Shechtman and Leichtentritt (2010) conducted a study with 266 children and adolescents in Israel. They found that bonding with the therapist (as measured with the bonding scale from the Working Alliance Inventory; Horvath & Greenberg, 1989) was a good predictor of process and outcome. They found that group functioning (i.e., interpersonal work, such as the child's active participation in the group as rated by the therapist), bonding (with both the therapist and the group), and therapeutic change were associated with social competence and reduced anxiety and aggression. You thought it interesting to consider that the group leader's responses of encouragement, interpretation, and self-disclosure were all found to be predictive of positive changes, whereas challenge was predictive of negative outcome (Shechtman & Leichtentritt, 2010). This fits with the earlier finding by Lieberman et al. (1973), who emphasized the importance of caring. In the groups with children and adolescents, when therapists were encouraging, offering interpretations, and modeling appropriate behavior through self-disclosure, the children benefited the most.

Another basic function from Lieberman et al. (1973) is termed *executive functioning*, which includes establishing boundaries in the group, such as setting rules, working with members to set goals, group management techniques, setting the subject matter, and norm setting. You reflect on how this leader function provides a framework for a group. It helps reduce ambiguity and lets group members know what is appropriate behavior (e.g., arriving on time and knowing appropriate topics for a given group), as well as what contributes to positive interactions (e.g., norms of using words instead of behaviors to express oneself).

You know that norm setting is a powerful tool in the group worker's repertoire. Norms can be set by highlighting certain responses that members make, asking questions to focus on one part of a member's experience (and not focusing on another), and wondering with the group why an action or topic wasn't commented on. Those are all more explicit ways to set norms, but you also know that the group leader's nonverbal behaviors can set norms. If you are warm, attentive to members' emotions, and use slight head nods to encourage a member to continue, then the group will likely pick up on these expressions and help create the climate. Alternatively, if you frown and turn to another member when the first member displays a certain behavior, such as disclosing about a dislike of the setting where the group is occurring, then this may shape the group into a climate where differences and conflicts are avoided and pushed underground. You know how key it is for the leader to shape norms into those that have a positive therapeutic impact.

One type of group with a higher level of structure is a *theme group*, a form of psychoeducation group. As you read more about them, theme groups seem to provide a way for a group worker to set the subject matter. Typically, theme groups use exercises and structure to move groups into the working stage (Drum & Knott, 2009). Theme groups can help in five different areas: acquiring skills, maintaining developmental statuses, life transitions, dealing or living with specific disorders, and maintaining recovery. *The Clearinghouse for Structured and Thematic Groups* (see http://cmhc.utexas.edu/clearinghouse/) provides an excellent resource for group workers looking for structured group resources, addressing topics such as assertiveness training, writing anxiety, surviving rape, overcoming addictive relationships, and self-nurturance.

Reading these studies on group workers' influence on groups makes you wonder what leader behaviors are effective for college student groups. You find a subset of the literature on the importance of cohesion that gives you some direction. Burlingame, McClendon, and Alonso (2011) provided an overview of the importance of cohesion. Within it, they list numerous behaviors that enhance group cohesion (see Table 3 in Burlingame et al., 2011). These are grouped into three categories: (a) group structuring (e.g., setting treatment expectations and establishing group procedures), (b) verbal interaction (e.g., modeling appropriate self-disclosure and encouraging positive feedback), and (c) creating and maintaining a therapeutic emotional climate (e.g., responding at an emotional level and using nonjudgmental language with members). These behaviors can be tracked using the Group Psychotherapy Intervention Rating Scale (GPIRS; Sternberg & Trijsburg, 2005). Chapman, Baker, Porter, Thayer, and Burlingame (2010) demonstrate concurrent validity of the GPIRS by comparing it to two other well-known leader rating methods.

You wonder if it would be helpful to analyze some of your own interventions in group using this scale. It might be possible for you to start videotaping some of your groups, and then you could watch it and rate your interventions. You decide to think about this further as you move into exploring the next research-supported change mechanism.

Structural Factors

The structural source of change includes treatment characteristics, such as group size, dose (number of groups and session length), and the sequencing of sessions. Kivlighan, London, and Miles (2011) compared coleadership with individual leadership of semistructured groups of adolescents. They found that the participants in co-led groups reported greater benefits from the therapy group than did the members in groups that were led by one group leader. They also found an interaction between group size and the type of leadership; in groups that were led by one group worker, as the group size increased, the ratings of avoidance increased and the ratings of engagement with the group decreased (Kivlighan et al., 2011). The group size ranged from 3 to 12 members, with an average of 6.58 members per group. However, in co-led groups, an increase in group size was related to lower levels of avoidance and an increased quality in group members' relationship with the group. They explained this by stating that "two leaders maximize the group's chance of utilizing the additional resources that increased membership brings" (p. 11). You decide to add this to your file for the support of coleadership. You know that in today's climate of increasing demand and fewer staff, it can be tempting to have only one leader for groups. However, this is an excellent example of the importance of having two leaders.

Formal Change Theory

In their original presentation of this model, Burlingame et al. (2004) reflected that "formal change theories typically originate from the individual rather than group psychotherapy literature" (p. 648). This observation can be seen in the large number of studies citing the general efficacy of different types of groups, including cognitive behavioral, psychodynamic, interpersonal, behavioral, and so on. Although too numerous to list here, you find the summary contained in their table (Table 14.1 in Burlingame et al., 2004) to be helpful, which highlights the many studies using group as a primary treatment for a range of disorders, including mood disorders, panic disorders, obsessive-compulsive disorder, social phobias, and eating disorders. The types of formal change theories included in this review were cognitive, cognitive behavioral, behavior, process-interactional, and psychodynamic therapy. More recently, Burlingame (2010) cited formal change theory as the one (out of these five sources of change) having the largest number of articles in the literature.

Burlingame (2010) and Burlingame et al. (2013) caution us about the impact of within-group dependence (e.g., members are nested within a group, but many statistical analyses in the group literature do not account for this condition). Consequently, there is an inflation of Type I error, meaning that many studies on group outcomes may be finding significant effects that are not true (e.g., false positives). It is worrisome to you that in their review of the research from the past decade, Burlingame et al. said regarding this effect: "Given that these effects were unaddressed in most studies, the above effectiveness conclusions are likely inflated; we just don't know how much" (p. 665). As you go back to the Kivlighan et al. (2011) article, you note that they specifically accounted for this. You are glad that the need to address this potential source of error appears to be gaining strength in the field.

In their latest review, Burlingame et al. (2013) pointed out that the evidence had accumulated enough to change their previous conclusions about a specific formal change theory (from Burlingame et al., 2004). For instance, in using groups as a primary treatment for obsessive-compulsive disorder, they stated that "there is now ample evidence for the efficacy of ERP [exposure and response prevention] and CBGT [cognitive behavioral group therapy] when compared to waitlist control" (p. 649). They also noted an "interesting trend" in "the integration of heretofore 'competing' approaches (e.g., CGBT + dynamic or IPIT) for the treatment of certain disorders" (p. 665). You are excited to see that the research is beginning to mirror what many practitioners already do—that is, work from an integrated treatment model.

Rather than looking further at the multitude of different studies examining each theoretical model, you wonder if you can take a common factors approach, similar to what has been done in the individual therapy literature (e.g., Wampold, 2001). Two of Lieberman et al.'s (1973) basic functions, *meaning attribution* and *emotional stimulation*, fall under the category of a common factors approach. A number of theories use cognitive understanding, or meaning attribution, in their key processes of change. Whether through cognitive behavioral therapy groups and understanding cognitive distortions or through interpersonal process groups with a focus on learning how one's interpersonal pattern is impacting others (and one's thoughts about oneself), you know that meaning attribution plays a key role in helping clients change in groups. You suspect that many group leaders use the emotional stimulation function, or the encouragement of expression and affective experiencing in group. However, as Yalom (2005) emphasized, catharsis or emotional expression alone is not enough. Members must develop a cognitive understanding that helps them make sense of the processes. And, of course, group leaders need to learn how to help members connect meaning with experience.

Another key process used in group work is fostering client awareness (American Group Psychotherapy Association, 2007). Only when group members gain knowledge about an issue, and an understanding of what contributes to its development or maintenance, can they work to change it. One reason why you value groups so highly is that they offer a wide range of ways for members to gain self-awareness, whether through didactic lectures, feedback from other group members on their interpersonal patterns, or reflecting on others' shared experiences in group.

Small-Group Processes

Burlingame et al. (2004) identified small-group processes as the "unique features of the group format that have been theoretically or empirically related to patient outcome" (p. 648). They highlight how these processes require "an appreciation of the *group* as a noun and how its collective properties can have strong effects on members" (p. 648). You realize that these dynamic processes, such as the therapeutic relationship in the group (i.e., cohesion), group development, and Yalom's (2005) therapeutic factors, were one of the initial appeals for you of getting into the group class during graduate school. Burlingame et al. (2013) reflected that too many of the authors of the randomized clinical trials they reviewed wondered about the role of group properties as contributing to the unaccounted variance. They issued a strongly worded caution as to the importance of this point: "We believe future progress *must* include measures of well-known group properties to at least rule them in or out as potential mechanisms of change" (p. 668; italics in original). To aid in the further development of the key group processes, they proposed a new model (see the Figure 5.1). You decide to investigate at least one element in each of their four categories.

Emergent Structure

Emergent structure provides information about how the group's "personality" is formed (Burlingame et al., 2013). One such structure that contributes to this is the group's development.

Group Development. Group development is considered as the patterns of growth and change that occur over the course of a group (Forsyth, 2006). Some models of group development can be characterized as *successive-stage models*, in which groups progress through each phase (Forsyth & Diederich, 2013). The classic example of this is Tuckman and Jensen's (1977) model of forming, storming, norming, performing, and adjourning. This model is familiar to you, as this is what you were taught in graduate school. Other models can be considered *cyclical models*, in which groups cycle through stages repeatedly (Forsyth & Diederich, 2013). Bion's (1961) assumptive cultures theory is an example of a cyclical model, in which groups shift between the work-group culture and one of the basic assumptive cultures. Another cyclical model you are familiar with is Bales's (1965) equilibrium model, in which groups shift from a task focus to a relationship focus. You have worked with your groups in the past to help balance a focus on tasks (such as working toward the goals of individual group members or the group as a whole) and on the relationship and emotional climate in the group. And yet other models are a combination of stage and cyclical models. You know that familiarity with stages of group development and group dynamics is crucial, as "a developmentally sensitive therapist can facilitate, hasten, retard, and exploit the processes that occur at each stage and those that move the group from one stage to the next" (Forsyth & Diederich, 2013).

One element of group development you have already added to your outline for group training is the use of structure early in the process. Although the

Figure 5.1   Group Structure—Anatomy

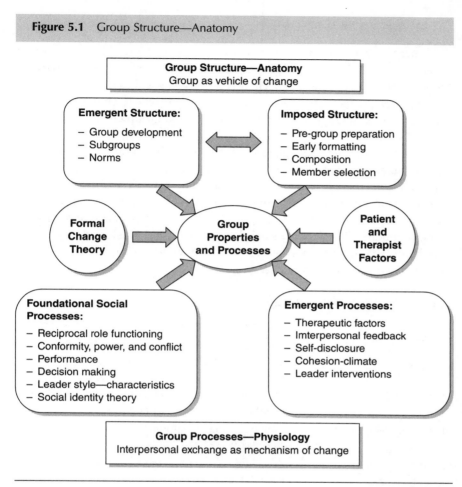

Group Structure—Anatomy
Group as vehicle of change

Emergent Structure:
- Group development
- Subgroups
- Norms

Imposed Structure:
- Pre-group preparation
- Early formatting
- Composition
- Member selection

Formal Change Theory

Group Properties and Processes

Patient and Therapist Factors

Foundational Social Processes:
- Reciprocal role functioning
- Conformity, power, and conflict
- Performance
- Decision making
- Leader style—characteristics
- Social identity theory

Emergent Processes:
- Therapeutic factors
- Imterpersonal feedback
- Self-disclosure
- Cohesion-climate
- Leader interventions

Group Processes—Physiology
Interpersonal exchange as mechanism of change

Source: Burlingame et al. (2013).

findings are complex, researchers have proposed that early group structure leads to less ambiguity, lower anxiety, and greater disclosure among group members (Burlingame, Fuhriman, & Johnson, 2001). Johnson (2009) provides a framework for using a semistructured approach for college students in interpersonal process groups. Typically, leaders of process groups avoid the use of structure, but you soon value Johnson's helpful tips on how to use this type of attention to structure and group development to great effectiveness within a semester system at a college or university (Forsyth & Diederich, in press).

Imposed Structure

Leader actions contribute to the imposed structure of a group. Imposed structure includes topics you have already reviewed, such as the impact of composition (e.g., as in the studies by Piper et al., 2007), pregroup preparation, and providing structure early in the time of a group (see Johnson, 2009).

Emergent Processes

Emergent processes are those that are a result of member and member/leader interactions, such as interpersonal feedback, self-disclosure, and processes that are byproducts of such interactions (e.g., cohesion, group climate, and therapeutic factors). You decide to focus your review on three key emergent processes: therapeutic factors, cohesion, and group climate.

Therapeutic Factors. Kivlighan and Holmes (2004) argue that one of Yalom's most influential contributions to the field is his work with therapeutic factors (originally called curative factors). Yalom's work has spanned decades and spawned many research papers, summarized in reviews by Kivlighan, Coleman, and Anderson (2000) and Kivlighan and Holmes (2004). Yalom's (2005) factors are defined in Table 5.1 below. A key change mechanism, cohesion, is further discussed below due to its prominence in the small-group processes literature.

Table 5.1   Therapeutic Factors

Factor	Description
Instillation of hope	Believing that group therapy will be helpful to the member
Universality	Perceiving that one is not alone, that other group members have similar experiences
Imparting information	Providing didactic information, advice, or suggestions
Altruism	Providing help to other members and benefiting from that experience
Corrective recapitulation of the primary family group	Having experiences in group that correctively relive earlier family conflicts
Development of socializing techniques	Learning social skills
Imitative behavior	Learning vicariously by observing the leader(s) and other members
Catharsis	Obtaining relief by releasing emotions
Existential factors	Grappling with the "givens" of life, such as death, isolation, freedom, and meaninglessness
Interpersonal learning	Gaining personal insight (input), working through interpersonal interactions, and having a corrective emotional experience
Group cohesiveness	The therapeutic relationship in the group, currently defined as having two dimensions: structure (the direction and function of the relationship) and quality of the relationship (Burlingame et al., 2011)

In reviewing a recent summary on therapeutic factors, you come across a recommendation by Kivlighan, Miles, and Paquin (2011) for future studies to stop simply examining group members' rankings of the importance of therapeutic factors (as more than 50 studies have already done so). Kivlighan et al. (2011) recommended that group workers tie findings from individual groups to a four-cluster typology to help understand how these therapeutic factors are linked to various group dimensions. Kivlighan and Holmes (2004) used factor analysis to define the following typology and relevant rankings of therapeutic factors:

- *Affective insight groups:* High levels of acceptance, catharsis, self-understanding, and interpersonal learning
- *Affective support groups:* High levels of instillation of hope, universality, and acceptance
- *Cognitive support groups:* High levels of vicarious learning and guidance, and low levels of self-understanding
- *Cognitive insight groups:* High levels of interpersonal learning, vicarious learning, and self-understanding, and low levels of guidance

Using these categories, you can imagine how a "Managing Low Mood" group using cognitive-behavioral techniques for students with depression would likely fall into the cognitive support group category. However, a general interpersonal process group, such as "Understanding Self and Others," might include the therapeutic factors from the affective insight group as primary. Despite the intuitive appeal of examining rankings of therapeutic factors across groups, Kivlighan et al. (2011) critiqued the existing research for failing to focus enough on the link from therapeutic factors to client outcome. They take this one step further and encourage researchers to focus on the interaction of how therapeutic factors operate for individual group members as well as for the group as a whole (and take into account the "nesting" of individual data within groups through statistical analysis; Kivlighan et al., 2011).

Cohesion. The therapeutic factor of cohesion is likely the most well-known of the small-group processes. The definitions of cohesion have changed over the years; an early definition by Yalom (1975) was "the attractiveness of a group for its members" (p. 46), and more recent descriptions reflect the theoretical and statistical complexity that has been applied to understanding cohesion. At its foundation, cohesion refers to the therapeutic relationships in group work. Burlingame et al. (2011) proposed two dimensions of cohesion: relationship structure and relationship quality. The structure refers to the direction and function of the relationship, such as the member-to-member and member-to-group relationships, whereas the quality refers to three factors: *positive bond* (the affective or emotional connections to the leader and other members), *positive work* (collaborative focus on tasks and goals), and *negative relationship* (empathic failure and conflict; Burlingame et al., 2011). These structural and quality factors are the result of a concerted research effort (e.g., Johnson, Burlingame, Olsen, Davies, & Gleave, 2005; Krogel, 2009) producing the Group Questionnaire (Burlingame, 2010).

The cohesion literature supports a positive relationship between cohesion and outcome (e.g., Burlingame et al., 2001; Evans & Dion, 1991), with a recent meta-analysis reporting a correlation between cohesion and outcome at $r = .25$, when outcome was measured by improvements in interpersonal functioning or symptom distress reduction (Burlingame et al., 2011). They found that group workers who focused on member-to-member interactions had higher cohesion to outcome findings. The relationship between cohesion and outcome was moderated by the following factors: treatment length (strongest when a group was longer than 12 sessions), age of client (stronger with younger group members, such as adolescents), and size of the group (strongest link between cohesion and outcome when groups had between five and nine members; Burlingame et al., 2011). A link between formal change theory and cohesion was found, leading Burlingame et al. (2011) to conclude that "this argues for cohesion being considered as an evidence-based relationship factor for groups using a cognitive-behavioral, psychodynamic, and interpersonal orientation" (p. 38). In reading a recent chapter on cohesion, you find that Marmarosh and Van Horn (2012) reported that higher cohesion resulted in a higher commitment to the group, also impacting factors such as attendance, disclosure, participation, and ability to tolerate conflict. You have long believed that effective groups require a strong sense of cohesion, and it's rewarding to see that the research supports this. You imagine, but cannot find explicit research to support, that positive member interconnections also contribute to effectiveness of task groups.

Given the solid foundation of support for cohesion as a change mechanism, you realize that the next step is for group workers to analyze the interactions between cohesion and other factors in the model by Burlingame et al. (2004). To do this, one study examined the interaction of clients' interpersonal style (as described in Carson, 1969, and Kiesler, 1983) and cohesion as related to outcome. Dinger and Schauenburg (2010) found that higher levels of cohesion were beneficial for all clients, but the impact of the change in cohesion over time varied depending on members' interpersonal style, specifically whether they were high on affiliation (too friendly) or low on affiliation (too hostile). You find it fascinating to consider that "increasing cohesion was especially helpful for patients with low affiliation, whereas a decrease of cohesion appeared more helpful for patients with high affiliation" (p. 26). In this way, Dinger and Schauenburg hypothesized that members who were hostile and cold benefited from being able to come closer and feel more connected to the group, but members who already struggled with being too close to others (i.e., too friendly) were able to gain control and distance in the group. You appreciate the nuances that this kind of research brings to thinking about interpersonal patterns in process groups and what is more helpful for specific clients.

Group Climate. Group climate has recently been described in three types: (a) *general,* which reflects "the general emotional atmosphere of the group"; (b) *factors,* which are "the product of interacting forces in a group"; and (c) *specific construct,* where "group climate is synonymous with a single construct, cohesion" (McClendon & Burlingame, 2012, p. 165). As you read this, you realize the particularly sticky situation, or complexity, that seems to characterize understandings of group climate. As evidence of this complexity, you see more than 20 definitions and terms used to describe group climate, with categorization into the three types given above (see Table 10.1 in McClendon & Burlingame, 2012).

There is a wealth of literature citing group climate as a change mechanism, likely due to the popularity of the Group Climate Questionnaire–Short Form (GCQ–S; MacKenzie, 1983). The GCQ–S is a self-report questionnaire containing three dimensions: engagement, avoidance, and conflict. McClendon and Burlingame (2012) summarized the support for the engagement scale as having strong and consistent findings related to outcome and process, and a moderate relationship (i.e., mixed results) with demonstrating patterns in groups over time, or group development. One example of this can be found in Ogrodniczuk and Piper's (2003) examination of climate and outcome in interpretive or supportive group therapy for clients with complicated grief. They found that engagement was significantly related to treatment outcome but that change in engagement across treatment was not related to outcome. They hypothesized that an early level of engagement (seen as early as after the fourth session) helps members "engage in the tasks of treatment and thus reap greater benefits from the group" (p. 72).

You know from some of your other reading that the avoiding scale of the GCQ–S has weaker findings than the engagement scale. McClendon and Burlingame (2011) summarized the findings on the avoiding scale by giving it a moderate-weak relationship to outcome and weak relationships to process and group development research. You recall seeing in the CORE-R Battery (Burlingame et al., 2006) a recommendation that the avoiding scale not be used for clinical use, due to its low internal consistency and poor factor structure in several studies (McClendon & Burlingame, 2012).

Finally, there is considerable overlap between climate and cohesion, both in the literature and in the statistical analyses. Recent studies—for instance, that of Johnson et al. (2005)—have examined four small-group processes (group climate, cohesion, alliance, and empathy) to explore underlying factors. As described above, their work has led to the development of the Group Questionnaire (Burlingame, 2010), which you hope will provide some theoretical construct clarity.

Foundational Social Processes

The foundational social processes are those that come from social and organizational psychology principles (Burlingame et al., 2013). Examples of these include social identity theory, conformity, power, and entitativity. Due to space, and because we think the term itself is just plain "fun," we will limit our discussion of social psychological foundations to just one—*entitativity*.

Entitativity. In your search to understand some of these social–psychological principles, you discover an impressive resource in Forsyth's (2010) book on group dynamics. He defines entitativity as "the extent to which individuals perceive an aggregation to be a unified group" (p. 27). As you read further, you reflect on how much this would apply to group, as you find that entitativity is influenced by members sharing a common fate (i.e., the extent to which individuals in the aggregate seem to experience interrelated outcomes), proximity cues (i.e., the distance between individuals in the aggregate), and similarity (i.e., the extent to which the individuals display the same behaviors or resemble one another). A group sharing a common fate, such as a task group whose members are strongly committed to accomplishing the same goal, is foundationally different from one where the members completely disagree about their purpose. A therapy group whose members choose to sit every session in close proximity and regularly address one another directly is different foundationally from one whose members maintain substantial physical distance and tend to avoid eye contact (proximity). Members of a counseling group expressing similarities might well focus on their commonalities in the early stages of a group, through a group leader working to foster elements of universality. Forsyth (2010, p. 27) pointed out, for instance, that when the Thomas theorem (i.e., what people perceive as being real is, in effect, real to them in its consequences) is applied to groups, members who believe their group is a "true" group will likely find it yielding important interpersonal consequences. Group leaders are wise to promote conditions in the group that are consistent with increasing entitativity among members.

Summary

As you finish your review, you reflect on change processes in task groups and in person-change groups. These sources all have an evidence base linking them to improvement. You feel confident that they provide key processes to attend to in working to help group members reach their goals—whether the goals be personal, interpersonal, or task oriented. Mix these ingredients together properly, and you will create groups that are in position to be effective, useful, and meaningful. As the group coordinator, charged with the mission to develop a plan for establishing comprehensive groups, you now are ready to move forward.

In this initial entry in the *Group Work Practice Kit,* we have attempted to lay a foundation for understanding group work by attending to basic concepts, supportive evidence for group effectiveness, best practices, multicultural and diversity dimensions, and how change occurs in these groups. In so doing, we have sought to answer the question: "What is group work?"

The books to follow in this kit will build from this introduction. Each one focuses on a key element of group work: How to design a group (Book 2), how to form a group (Book 3), how to establish conditions for change (Book 4), how to select and apply change strategies (Book 5), how to learn from the group experience (Book 6), and how to evaluate groups (Book 7); the final two books address how groups can be applied in the community (Book 8) and in schools (Book 9).

We hope you have found this first book to be of value, as we hope you will the subsequent books in this kit.

Learning Exercises

1. *Matching therapeutic factors and giving examples*

   a. Match: Draw lines to connect each therapeutic factor listed with its correct sentiment.

SAMPLE THERAPEUTIC FACTOR	DEFINITION
Universality	"Helping you helped me."
Imparting information	"I didn't realize I was not alone."
Catharsis	"It's possible for us all to change."
Altruism	"First, I'll define *feedback*."
Instillation of hope	"Getting this out felt good."

   b. Personalize: Meet with a partner to compare your matches and determine correct relationships. Then, personalize each match by giving an example of how you have experienced each therapeutic factor in groups (15 minutes).

2. *Becoming acquainted, developing connections*

   Forming connections among members is a necessary precondition for effective group work of all kinds. This exercise in three parts builds on an existing group. The object is to work together to do one or all three activities (15 minutes per activity).

   a. Create a descriptive name that captures the group's essence.

   b. Pick a theme song that fits (e.g., "We Are the Champions" or "Take It to the Limit")

   c. Prepare a presentation to be given to other groups that are doing the same thing.

3. *Your own group leader functions*

   Apply the Lieberman, Yalom, and Miles (1973) group leadership functions to yourself (even if you have only limited experience in leading groups). Consider your involvement with others across a variety of situations (family gathering, work and class settings, support groups, parties, etc.). Write an estimate of where you see yourself in relation to each function, followed by a paragraph indicating how you intend to integrate them.

   a. Self-estimate of group leadership function

      Caring: _____

      _____

      _____.

      Meaning attribution: _____

      _____

      _____.

      Emotional stimulation: _____

      _____

      _____.

      Executive functioning: _____

      _____

      _____.

   b. How would you like to see these four functions relating to each other in your own practice?

      _____

      _____

      _____

      _____.

4. You recall at the start of this chapter that we pointed out how the information on change processes (indeed, about group work in general) is tied most closely to person-change groups. We indicated some particular change factors associated with task groups, and we made the point that the change sources commonly connected with person-change groups hold value for task groups, too. It is important, for instance, that a task group, such as a committee, develop a structure for proceeding, create a positive working atmosphere, and that a task group leader help members function effectively and meaningfully.

To assist your understanding of how change occurs within task groups, take about 30 minutes to complete the final exercise in this book:

a. Describe a task group in enough detail to provide a fairly concrete context.

  _____

  _____

  _____.

b. Select three change factors (these could be drawn from the discussion of task groups at the start of this chapter or from the change processes commonly associated with person-change groups) and indicate how each one can be valuable in helping the task group function as an effective team:

  Change Factor #1: _____

  _____

  _____.

  Change Factor #2: _____

  _____

  _____.

  Change Factor #3: _____

  _____

  _____

c. Discuss with a partner what you developed, specifically identifying the change factors you chose and how each might work.

References

American Counseling Association. (2013). 20/20: A vision for the future of counseling. Retrieved from http://www.counseling.org/knowledge-center/20-20-a-vision-for-the-future-of-counseling

American Group Psychotherapy Association. (2007). *Practice guidelines for group psychotherapy: A cross-theoretical guide to developing and leading psychotherapy groups.* New York: Author. Retrieved July 24, 2011, from http://agpa.org/guidelines/index.html

Arredondo, P., Toporek, R., Pack Brown, S., Sanchez, J., Locke, D. C., Sanchez, J., et al. (1996). Operationalization of the multicultural counseling competencies. *Journal of Multicultural Counseling & Development, 24,* 42–78.

Association for the Advancement of Social Work with Groups. (2005). *Standards for social work practice with groups* (2nd ed.). Alexandria, VA: Author. Retrieved from http://www.aaswg.org/standards-social-work-practice-with-groups

Bales, R. F. (1965). The equilibrium problem in small groups. In A. P. Hare, E. F. Borgatta, & R. F. Bales (Eds.), *Small groups: Studies in social interaction* (Rev. ed., pp. 444–483). New York: Knopf.

Barlow, S. (2012). An application of the competency model to group-specialty practice. *Professional Psychology: Research and Practice, 43,* 442–451. doi:10.1037/a0029090

Barlow, S. H., Burlingame, G. M., & Fuhriman, A. (2000). Therapeutic applications of groups: From Pratt's "thought control classes" to modern group psychotherapy. *Group Dynamics: Theory, Research, and Practice, 4*(1), 115–134.

Barlow, S., Fuhriman, A., & Burlingame, G. (2005). The history of group practice: A century of knowledge. In S. Wheelan (Ed.), *Handbook of group research and practice* (pp. 39–64). Thousand Oaks, CA: Sage.

Bion, W. (1961). *Experiences in groups.* New York: Basic Books.

Boewe, M., & McWhirter, J. J. (2002). *ART: Anxiety Reduction Training—Trainer's manual and student workbook.* Unpublished treatment manual manuscript, Arizona State University, Tempe, AZ.

Brown, N. W. (2003). Conceptualizing process. *International Journal of Group Psychotherapy, 53*(2), 225–244.

Burlingame, G. M. (2010). Small group treatments: Introduction to special section. *Psychotherapy Research, 20*(1), 1–7.

Burlingame, G. M., & Beecher, M. E. (2008). New directions and resources in group psychotherapy: Introduction to the issue. *Journal of Clinical Psychology, 64*(11), 1197–1205.

Burlingame, G. M., Earnshaw, D., Hoag, M., Barlow, S. H., Richardson, E. J., Donnell, I., et al. (2002). A systematic program to enhance clinician group skills in an inpatient psychiatric hospital. *International Journal of Group Psychotherapy, 52,* 555–587.

Burlingame, G. M., Fuhriman, A., & Johnson, J. E. (2001). Cohesion in group psychotherapy. *Psychotherapy: Theory, Research, Practice, Training, 38*(4), 373–379.

Burlingame, G. M., Fuhriman, A., & Mosier, J. (2003). The differential effectiveness of group psychotherapy: A meta-analytic perspective. *Group Dynamics: Theory, Research, and Practice, 7*(1), 3–12.

Burlingame, G. M., MacKenzie, K. R., & Strauss, B. (2004). Small-group treatment: Evidence for effectiveness and mechanisms of change. In M. Lambert (Eds.), *Bergin and Garfield's handbook of psychotherapy and behavior change* (5th ed., 647–696). New York: John Wiley.

Burlingame, G. M., McClendon, D. T., & Alonso, J. (2011). Cohesion in group therapy. *Psychotherapy, 48*(1), 34–42.

Burlingame, G. M., Strauss, B., & Joyce, A. S. (2013). Change mechanisms and effectiveness of small group treatments. In M. J. Lambert (Ed.), *Bergin and Garfield's handbook of psychotherapy and behavior change* (6th ed., pp. 640–689). New York: John Wiley.

Burlingame, G. M., Strauss, B., Joyce, A., MacNair-Semands, R., MacKenzie, K. R., Ogrodniczuk, J., et al. (2006). *CORE battery–revised: An assessment tool kit for promoting optimal group selection, process and outcome.* New York: American Group Psychotherapy Association.

Burnes, T. R., & Ross, K. L. (2010). Applying social justice to oppression and marginalization in group process: Interventions and strategies for group counselors. *Journal for Specialists in Group Work, 35*(2), 169–176.

Carson, R. C. (1969). *Interaction concepts of personality.* Oxford, UK: Aldine.

Chapman, C. L., Baker, E. L., Porter, G., Thayer, S. D., & Burlingame, G. M. (2010). Rating group therapist interventions: The validation of the Group Psychotherapy Intervention Rating Scale. *Group Dynamics: Theory, Research, and Practice, 14*(1), 15–31.

Chapman, C. L., Burlingame, G. M., Gleave, R., Rees, F., Beecher, M., & Porter, G. S. (2012). Clinical prediction in group psychotherapy. *Psychotherapy Research, 22*(6), 673–681.

Choate, L. H., & Henson, A. (2003). Group work with adult survivors of childhood abuse and neglect: A psychoeducational approach. *Journal for Specialists in Group Work, 28,* 106–121.

Clanton Harpine, E. (2013). Prevention groups. In R. Conyne & A. Horne (Eds.), *Prevention practice kit.* Thousand Oaks, CA: Sage.

Cohen, S., & Bailey, D. (1997). What makes teams work: Group effectiveness research from the shop floor to the executive suite. *Journal of Management, 23,* 239–290.

Conyne, R. (1989). *How personal growth and task groups work.* Newbury Park, CA: Sage.

Conyne, R. (2004). *Preventive counseling: Helping people to become empowered in systems and settings* (2nd ed.). New York: Brunner-Routledge.

Conyne, R. (2010). *Prevention program development and evaluation: An incidence reduction, culturally relevant approach.* Thousand Oaks, CA: Sage.

Conyne, R. (2011a). Group counseling. In E. Altmaier & J. C. Hansen (Eds.), *Oxford handbook of counseling psychology* (pp. 611–646). New York: Oxford University Press.

Conyne, R. (Ed.). (2011b). *Oxford handbook of group counseling.* New York: Oxford University Press.

Conyne, R. (2013). *Group work leadership: An introduction for helpers.* Thousand Oaks, CA: Sage.

Conyne, R., & Harding, E. (1976). Environmental assessment inventory–group. *Together, 1,* 26–31.

Conyne, R., Newmeyer, M., & Crowell, J. (2008). *Group techniques: How to use them more purposefully.* Upper Saddle River, NJ: Pearson.

Conyne, R., Rapin, L., & Rand, J. (1997). A model for leading task groups. In H. Forester-Miller & J. Kottler (Eds.), *Issues and challenges for group practitioners* (pp. 117–131). Denver, CO: Love.

Conyne, R., Wilson, F. R., & Ward, D. (1997). *Comprehensive group work: What it means and how to teach it.* Alexandria, VA: American Counseling Association.

Corey, G., Corey, M. S., & Haynes, R. (2006). *Groups in action: Evolution and challenges* [DVD and workbook]. Belmont, CA: Brooks/Cole, Cengage Learning.

DeLucia-Waack, J., & Donigian, J. (2004). *The practice of multicultural group work: Visions and perspectives from the field.* Pacific Grove, CA: Wadsworth.

DeLucia-Waack, J., Gerrity, D., Kalodner, C., & Riva, M. (Eds.). (2004). *Handbook of group counseling and psychotherapy.* Thousand Oaks, CA: Sage.

Dinger, U., & Schauenburg, H. (2010). Effects of individual cohesion and patient interpersonal style on outcome in psychodynamically oriented inpatient group psychotherapy. *Psychotherapy Research, 20*(1), 22–29.

Drum, D. J., & Knott, J. E. (2009). Theme groups at thirty. *International Journal of Group Psychotherapy, 59*(4), 491–510.

Eason, E. A. (2009). Diversity and group theory, practice, and research. *International Journal of Group Psychotherapy, 59*(4), 563–574.

Evans, C. R., & Dion, K. L. (1991). Group cohesion and performance: A meta-analysis. *Small Group Research, 22,* 175–186.

Fair, C. A., & McWhirter, J. J. (2002). *BLOCKS: Building Lives on Cooperative Knowledge Skills—Trainer's manual and student workbook.* Unpublished treatment manual manuscript, Arizona State University Tempe, AZ.

Falls, L. (2009). Group work, types of. In American Counseling Association (Ed.), *The ACA encyclopedia of counseling* (pp. 251–254). Alexandria, VA: Author.

Ferguson, C. J. (2009). An effect size primer: A guide for clinicians and researchers. *Professional Psychology: Research and Practice, 40,* 532–538.

Forsyth, D. (2006). *Group dynamics.* Belmont, CA: Thomson Wadsworth.

Forsyth, D. (2010). *Group dynamics* (5th ed.). Belmont, CA: Wadsworth.

Forsyth, D. (2011). The nature and significance of groups. In R. Conyne (Ed.), *Oxford handbook of group counseling* (pp. 19–35). New York: Oxford University Press.

Forsyth, D., & Diederich, L. T. (2013). Group dynamics and development. In J. DeLucia-Waack, D. Gerrity, C. Kalodner, & M. Riva (Eds.), *Handbook of group counseling and psychotherapy* (2nd ed.). Thousand Oaks, CA: Sage.

Gazda, G. M. (1978). *Group counseling: A developmental approach.* Boston: Allyn & Bacon.

Gilboy, S. F., McWhirter, J. J., & Wallace, R. (2002). *SOAR: Students Optimism and Resiliency Program: Building on strength—Trainer's manual and student workbook*. Unpublished treatment manual manuscript, Arizona State University, Tempe, AZ.

Hackman, R. (2011, June 7). Six common misperceptions about teamwork. *HBR Blog Network*. Boston: Harvard Business Review.

Herrmann, D. S., & McWhirter, J. J. (2001). *SCARE: Student Created Aggression Replacement Education*. Dubuque, IA: Kendall/Hunt.

Hoffmann, L. L., Gleave, R. L., Burlingame, G. M., & Jackson, A. P. (2009). Exploring interactions of improvers and deteriorators in the group therapy process: A qualitative analysis. *International Journal of Group Psychotherapy, 59*(2), 179–197.

Hogg, M., Hohman, Z., & Rivera, J. (2008, April). Why do people join groups? Three motivational accounts from social psychology. *Social & Personality Psychology Compass, 2,* 1269–1280.

Horvath, A. O., & Greenberg, L. S. (1989). Development and validation of the Working Alliance Inventory. *Journal of Counseling Psychology, 36*(2), 223–233.

Hulse-Killacky, D., Killacky, J., & Donigian, J. (2001). *Making task groups work in your world*. Upper Saddle River, NJ: Merrill Prentice Hall.

Hurt, B. (2006). *Hip-hop: Beyond beats and rhymes*. Northhampton, MA: Media Education Foundation.

Johnson, C. V. (2009). A process-oriented group model for university students: A semi-structured approach. *International Journal of Group Psychotherapy, 59*(4), 511–528.

Johnson, I. H., Torres, J. S., Coleman, V. D., & Smith, M. C. (1995). Issues and strategies in leading culturally diverse counseling groups. *Journal for Specialists in Group Work, 20*(3), 143–150.

Johnson, J. E., Burlingame, G. M., Olsen, J. A., Davies, D. R., & Gleave, R. L. (2005). Group climate, cohesion, alliance, and empathy in group psychotherapy: Multilevel structural equation models. *Journal of Counseling Psychology, 52,* 310–321.

Kiesler, D. J. (1983). The 1982 interpersonal circle: A taxonomy for complementarity in human transactions. *Psychological Review, 90,* 185–214.

Kipper, D. A., & Ritchie, T. D. (2003). The effectiveness of psychodramatic techniques: A meta-analysis. *Group Dynamics: Theory, Research, and Practice, 7*(1), 13–25.

Kivlighan, D. M., Jr., Coleman, M. N., & Anderson, D. C. (2000). Process, outcome and methodology in group counseling research. In S. D. Brown & R. W. Lent (Eds.), *Handbook of counseling psychology* (3rd ed., pp. 767–796). New York: John Wiley.

Kivlighan, D., Jr., & Holmes, S. (2004). The importance of therapeutic factors. In J. DeLucia-Waack, D. Gerrity, C. Kalodner, & M. Riva (Eds.), *Handbook of group counseling and psychotherapy* (pp. 23–36). Thousand Oaks, CA: Sage.

Kivlighan, D. M., Jr., London, K., & Miles, J. R. (2012). Are two heads better than one? The relationship between number of group leaders and group members, and group climate and group member benefit from therapy. *Group Dynamics: Theory, Research, and Practice, 16*(1), 1–13.

Kivlighan, D., Jr., Miles, J., & Paquin, J. (2011). Therapeutic factors in group counseling: Asking new questions. In R. Conyne (Ed.), *Oxford handbook of group counseling* (pp. 121–136). New York: Oxford University Press.

Korda, L. J., & Pancrazio, J. J. (1989). Limiting negative outcome in group practice. *Journal for Specialists in Group Work, 14*(2), 112–120.

Kormanski, C. (1999). *The team: Explorations in group process*. Denver, CO: Love.

Kösters, M., Burlingame, G. M., Nachtigall, C., & Strauss, B. (2006). A meta-analytic review of the effectiveness of inpatient group psychotherapy. *Group Dynamics: Theory, Research, and Practice, 10*(2), 146–163.

Krogel, J. (2009). *The Group Questionnaire: A new measure of the group relationship*. Unpublished doctoral dissertation, Brigham Young University, Provo, UT.

Lambert, M. J., Burlingame, G. M., Umphress, V., Hansen, N. B., Vemeersch, D. A., Clouse, G. C., et al. (1996). The reliability and validity of the Outcome Questionnaire. *Clinical Psychology & Psychotherapy, 3*(4), 249–258.

Lee, M. W., Hunter, M., Goss, R., Jr., & Bock, R. C. (1997). *The color of fear* [DVD]. Oakland, CA: Stir-Fry Seminars and Consulting.

Lewis, J., Arnold, M. S., House, R., & Toporek, R. (2003). *Advocacy competencies*. Retrieved from http://www.counseling.org/docs/competencies/advocacy_competencies.pdf?sfvrsn=3

Lieberman, M. A., Yalom, I. D., & Miles, M. B. (1973). *Encounter groups: First facts*. New York: Basic Books.

MacKenzie, K. R. (1983). The clinical application of a group climate measure. In R. R. Dies & K. R. MacKenzie (Eds.), *Advances in group psychotherapy: Integrating research and practice* (pp. 159–170). New York: International Universities Press.

MacKenzie, K. R. (2001). Group psychotherapy. In W. J. Livesley (Ed.), *Handbook of personality disorders* (pp. 497–526). New York: Guilford Press.

MacNair-Semands, R. R. (2002). Predicting attendance and expectations for group therapy. *Group Dynamics: Theory, Research, and Practice, 6*(3), 219–228.

Marmarosh, C. L., & Van Horn, S. M. (2012). Cohesion in counseling and psychotherapy groups. In R. Conyne (Ed.), *The Oxford handbook of group counseling* (pp. 137–163). New York: Oxford University Press.

McClendon, D. T., & Burlingame, G. M. (2012). Group climate: Construct in search of clarity. In R. Conyne (Ed.), *The Oxford handbook of group counseling* (pp. 164–181). New York: Oxford University Press.

McWhirter, P. T., & McWhirter, J. J. (2010). Community and school violence and risk reduction: Empirically supported prevention. *Group Dynamics: Theory, Research, and Practice, 14*(3), 242–256.

Mirandé, A. (1997). *Hombres y machos: Masculinity and Latino culture*. Boulder, CO: Westview Press.

Morgan, R. D., & Flora, D. B. (2002). Group psychotherapy with incarcerated offenders: A research synthesis. *Group Dynamics: Theory, Research, and Practice, 6*(3), 203–218.

Newman-Carlson, D., & Horne, A. M. (2004). Bully Busters: A psychoeducational intervention for reducing bullying behavior in middle school students. *Journal of Counseling & Development, 82*(3), 259–267.

Newmeyer, M. (2009). Group work training. In American Counseling Association (Ed.), *The ACA encyclopedia of counseling* (pp. 250–251). Alexandria, VA: Author.

Oei, T. P. S., & Browne, A. (2006). Components of group processes: Have they contributed to the outcome of mood and anxiety disorder patients in a group cognitive-behavior therapy program? *American Journal of Psychotherapy, 60*, 53–70.

Ogrodniczuk, J. S., Joyce, A. S., Lynd, L. D., Piper, W. E., Steinberg, P. I., & Richardson, K. (2008). Predictors of premature termination of day treatment for personality disorder. *Psychotherapy and Psychosomatics, 77*(6), 365–371.

Ogrodniczuk, J. S., & Piper, W. E. (2003). The effect of group climate on outcome in two forms of short-term group therapy. *Group Dynamics: Theory, Research, and Practice, 7*(1), 64–76.

Ogrodniczuk, J. S., Piper, W. E., Joyce, A. S., McCallum, M., & Rosie, J. S. (2003). NEO-five factor personality traits as predictors of response to two forms of group psychotherapy. *International Journal of Group Psychotherapy, 53*(4), 417–442.

Ogrodniczuk, J. S., Piper, W. E., McCallum, M., Joyce, A. S., & Rosie, J. S. (2002). Interpersonal predictors of group therapy outcome for complicated grief. *International Journal of Group Psychotherapy, 52*(4), 511–535.

Olweus, D., & Limber, S. (2002). *Blueprints for violence prevention: Bullying prevention program.* Boulder: Center for the Study of Violence Prevention, University of Colorado at Boulder.

Otto, M., Pollack, M., & Maki, K. (2000). Empirically supported treatments for panic disorder. *Journal of Consulting and Clinical Psychology, 68*(4), 556–563.

Payne, K. T., & Marcus, D. K. (2008). The efficacy of group psychotherapy for older adult clients: A meta-analysis. *Group Dynamics: Theory, Research, and Practice, 12*(4), 268–278.

Piper, W. E., Ogrodniczuk, J. S., Joyce, A. S., Weideman, R., & Rosie, J. S. (2007). Group composition and group therapy for complicated grief. *Journal of Consulting and Clinical Psychology, 75*(1), 116–125.

Ratts, M., Anthony, L., & Santos, K. N. (2010). The dimensions of social justice model: Transforming traditional group work into a socially just framework. *Journal for Specialists in Group Work, 35*, 160–168. doi:10.1080/0193392 1003705974

Ridley, C. R. (2005). *Overcoming unintentional racism in counseling and therapy: A practitioner's guide to intentional intervention* (2nd ed.). Thousand Oaks, CA: Sage.

Roberge, P., Marchand, A., Reinharz, D., & Savard, P. (2008). Cognitive-behavioral treatment for panic disorder with agoraphobia. *Behavior Modification, 32*, 333–351.

Sapia, J. L. (2001). Using groups for the prevention of eating disorders among college women. *Journal for Specialists in Group Work, 26*, 256–266.

Schwarz, R. (2002). *The skilled facilitator: A comprehensive resource for consultants, facilitators, manager, trainers, and coaches.* San Francisco: Jossey-Bass.

Shechtman, Z., & Leichtentritt, J. (2010). The association of process with outcomes in child group therapy. *Psychotherapy Research, 20*(1), 8–21.

Silko, L. M. (2000). *Gardens in the dunes: A novel.* New York: Simon & Schuster.

Simmons, A. S. (2006). *NO! The rape documentary.* Philadelphia: AfroLez Productions.

Singh, A. A., Merchant, N., Skudrzyk, B., & Ingene, D. (2012). *Association for Specialists in Group Work: Multicultural and social justice competence principles for group workers.* Retrieved from http://www.asgw.org/pdf/ASGW_MC_SJ_Priniciples_Final_ASGW.pdf

Society of Group Psychology and Group Psychotherapy. (2013). *Group resources.* Retrieved from http://www.apadivisions.org/division-49/about/resources/index.aspx

Sternberg, S., & Trijsburg, W. (2005). *The relationship between therapeutic interventions and therapeutic outcome.* Unpublished manuscript.

Taft, C. T., Murphy, C. M., Musser, P. H., & Remington, N. A. (2004). Personality, interpersonal, and motivational predictors of the working alliance in group cognitive-behavioral therapy for partner violent men. *Journal of Consulting and Clinical Psychology, 72*(2), 349–354.

Thomas, R. V., & Pender, D. A. (2008). *Association for Specialists in Group Work: Best practice guidelines 2007 revisions.* Retrieved from http://asgw.org/pdf/Best_Practices.pdf

Tuckman, B. W., & Jensen, M. A. C. (1977). Stages of small-group development revisited. *Group & Organization Management, 2*(4), 419–427.

Wampold, B. E. (2001). *The great psychotherapy debate: Models, methods, and findings.* Mahwah, NJ: Lawrence Erlbaum.

Ward, D. (2011). Definition. In R. Conyne (Ed.), *Oxford handbook of group counseling* (pp. 36–51). New York: Oxford University Press.

Weisbord, M. (1978). *Organizational diagnosis.* Reading, MA: Addison-Wesley.

Wheelan, S. (2004). Groups in the workplace. In J. L. DeLucia-Waack, D. Gerrity, C. Kalodner, & M. Riva (Eds.), *Group handbook of group counseling and psychotherapy* (pp. 401–413). Thousand Oaks, CA: Sage.

Whiston, S. C., & Li, P. (2011). Meta-analysis: A systematic method for synthesizing counseling research. *Journal of Counseling & Development, 89,* 273–281.

Wilson, F. R., Rapin, L. S., & Haley-Banez, L. (2000). *Professional standards for the training of group workers.* Retrieved from http://asgw.org/pdf/training_standards.pdf

Wise, T. (2011). *White like me: Reflections on race from a privileged son* (Rev. ed.). New York: Soft Skull Press.

Yalom, I. D. (1975). *The theory and practice of group psychotherapy* (2nd ed.). New York: Basic Books.

Yalom, I. D. (with Leszcz, M.). (2005). *The theory and practice of group psychotherapy* (5th ed.). New York: Basic Books.

Index

About the Authors _____

Robert K. Conyne, PhD, Professor Emeritus at the University of Cincinnati and William A. Allen Endowed Chair and Distinguished Professor, 2013–2014, at Seattle University, is a licensed psychologist, clinical counselor, and Fellow of the Association for Specialists in Group Work (ASGW) and the American Psychological Association (APA). He has compiled 40 years of professional experience as a university professor and department head, counselor, administrator, consultant, and trainer. Bob has received many awards, including the Eminent Career Award from ASGW; the Lifetime Achievement Award in Prevention from the APA's Society of Counseling Psychology; the Distinguished Alumni Award of Distinction from Purdue University; and a Soros International Scholar. He was president of the APA's Division of Group Psychology and Group Psychotherapy and also of the American Counseling Association's Association for Specialists in Group Work. With more than 200 scholarly publications and presentations, including 14 books in his areas of expertise (group work, prevention, and ecological counseling), along with broad international consultation in these areas—most recently with U.S. military personnel—Bob is recognized as an expert in working with people and systems. With colleague (and wife), Lynn S. Rapin, PhD, he also helps people plan and prepare psychologically for their upcoming retirement, using the holistic approach they developed, "Charting Your Personal Future." *The Prevention Practice Kit* (coedited with A. Horne, 2013) and his text *Group Work Leadership: An Introduction for Helpers* with SAGE are his most recent efforts, preceded by the *Oxford Handbook of Group Counseling* (2011) and 12 other books. Bob will assume a special position at Seattle University for 2013–2014 as the William A. Allen Endowed Chair and Distinguished Professor. When not working, Bob and Lynn—as often as possible with their children, Suzanne (married to Pete) and Zack—can be found traveling or enjoying life at their Northern Ontario cottage with their dog, Lucy.

Leann Terry Diederich, PhD, group therapy coordinator at the Center for Counseling and Psychological Services at The Pennsylvania State University, is a licensed psychologist. She is a member of the Association for Specialists in Group Work. She is also Member-at-Large for the Society of Group

Psychology and Group Psychotherapy (Division 49 of the American Psychological Association) and focuses on the needs of early-career professionals. She is active in providing group work training, both locally and at the national level, through presentations at the American Group Psychotherapy Association annual conference. She is a firm believer in the value of sharing group resources, promoting group work, and mentoring. As part of striving toward a balanced life, she enjoys gardening, horseback riding, and ballroom dancing.